Ranger Rick's NatureScope

INCREDIBLE
INSECTS

National Wildlife Federation

**LEARNING
TRIANGLE
PRESS**

*Connecting
kids, parents, and teachers
through learning*

An imprint of McGraw-Hill
New York San Francisco Washington, D.C. Auckland Bogotá Caracas
Lisbon London Madrid Mexico City Milan Montreal New Delhi
San Juan Singapore Sydney Tokyo Toronto

Library of Congress Cataloging-in-Publication Data

Incredible Insects/National Wildlife Federation.
p. cm.—(Ranger Rick's naturescope)
Includes bibliographical references (p.).
ISBN 0-07-047102-9 (pbk.)
1. Insects—Study and teaching—Activity programs. 2. Insects—
Study and teaching (Elementary). I. National Wildlife Federation.
II. Series.
QL468.5.I535 1998   97-36216
372.3'57—dc21   CIP

McGraw-Hill

A Division of The McGraw-Hill Companies

NATIONAL WILDLIFE FEDERATION®

1 2 3 4 5 6 7 8 9 JDL/JDL 9 0 3 2 1 0 9 8

ISBN 0-07-047102-9

NatureScope® was originally conceived by National Wildlife Federation's School Programs Editorial Staff, under the direction of Judy Braus, Editor. Special thanks to all of the Editorial Staff, Scientific, Educational Consultants and Contributors who brought this series of eighteen publications to life.

NATIONAL WILDLIFE FEDERATION EDITORIAL STAFF
Creative Services Manager: Sharon Schiliro
Editor, Ranger Rick® magazine: Gerry Bishop
Director, Classroom-related Programs: Margaret Tunstall
Contributors: Donald M. Silver, Patricia J. Wynne

McGRAW-HILL EDP STAFF
Acquisitions Editor: Judith Terrill-Breuer
Editorial Supervisor: Patricia V. Amoroso
Production Supervisor: Clare Stanley
Designer: York Production Services
Cover Design: David Saylor

RRNS

OTHER TITLES IN *RANGER RICK'S NATURESCOPE*

AMAZING MAMMALS, PART I
AMAZING MAMMALS, PART II
ASTRONOMY ADVENTURES
BIRDS, BIRDS, BIRDS
DIGGING INTO DINOSAURS
DISCOVERING DESERTS
DIVING INTO OCEANS
ENDANGERED SPECIES: WILD & RARE

GEOLOGY: THE ACTIVE EARTH
LET'S HEAR IT FOR HERPS
POLLUTION: PROBLEMS & SOLUTIONS
RAIN FORESTS: TROPICAL TREASURES
TREES ARE TERRIFIC!
WADING INTO WETLANDS
WILD ABOUT WEATHER
WILD & CRAFTY

GOAL

Ranger Rick's NatureScope is a creative education series dedicated to inspiring in children an understanding and appreciation of the natural world while developing the skills they will need to make responsible decisions about the environment.

A Close-Up Look At Incredible Insects

There's a lot in these 96 pages of *Incredible Insects*. We hope this introduction will give you the overview you need to decide how it can best fit your needs.

If you look at the Table of Contents, you can see we've divided the study of insects into five main chapters, each of which deals with a broad ecology or natural history theme, followed by a craft section and an appendix.

Each of the five chapters includes *background information* that explains concepts and vocabulary, *activities* that relate to the chapter theme, and *Copycat Pages* that reinforce many of the concepts introduced in the activities.

You can choose single activity ideas or teach each section as a unit. Either way, each activity stands by itself and includes teaching objectives, a list of materials needed, suggested age levels, subjects covered, and a step-by-step explanation of how to do the activity. (The objectives, materials, age groups, and subjects are highlighted in the left-hand margin for easy reference.)

AGE GROUPS

The suggested age groups are:

- Primary (grades K-2)
- Intermediate (grades 3-5)
- Advanced (grades 6-8)

Each chapter begins with primary activities and ends with intermediate or advanced activities. But don't feel bound by the grade levels we suggest. You'll be able to adapt many of these activities to fit your particular age group and needs.

OUTDOOR ACTIVITIES

One of the most exciting ways for children to learn about insects is for them to see and study insects in their natural habitats. So we've tried to include at least one outdoor activity in each chapter.

These are coded in the chapters in which they appear with this symbol:

COPYCAT PAGES

The Copycat Pages supplement the activities and include ready-to-copy games, puzzles, coloring pages, worksheets, and mazes. *Answers to all Copycat Pages are on page 94.*

WHAT'S AT THE END

The sixth section, *Crafty Corner,* will give you some art and craft ideas that complement many of the activities in the first five sections. And the last section, the *Appendix,* is loaded with reference suggestions that include books, records, and films. The Appendix also has insect questions and answers, ideas for making insect traps and nets, and suggestions for attracting insects.

FITTING IT ALL IN

We've tried to combine the science activities in *Incredible Insects* with language arts, history, creative writing, physical education, social studies, math, and art activities to make this booklet as useful as possible. For example, the "Populations Count" activity is a good math activity, as well as a good science activity. And the "Interview with a Gypsy Moth" is a creative drama activity that can be used with or without other insect activities.

If you plan to do an entire unit on insects, *Incredible Insects* can be your major source of background information and activity ideas. But if you think you have time to use only a few of the activity ideas, check the objectives and subjects to see which ones will complement what you're already doing.

We hope *Incredible Insects* will provide you with a source of activity ideas and project suggestions that you can use over and over again with your groups.

SAFETY NOTES

As we mentioned before, many children and adults are afraid of insects. Most of this fear is unfounded because most insects are harmless to people.

But there are exceptions, and we want to make sure that you do take necessary safety precautions when you're outside with your children.

Bees and wasps are the main troublemakers. The females can sting, but usually won't unless provoked. Warn your group not to collect bees or wasps or anything that looks like a bee or wasp.

If someone in your group is allergic to stings, stay away from fields—this is where most bees and wasps live and feed. Collect in the woods or by a pond or stream.

Also remind your group not to pick up insects with their hands unless they know the insect is harmless. For example, crickets, butterflies, moths, cockroaches, flies, and many other insects won't hurt you at all. (For those insects that you're not sure about, use a collecting jar to capture them so that you can take a closer look without getting stung or bitten.)

With a little common sense, your outdoor trips will be exciting and rewarding for both you and your group!

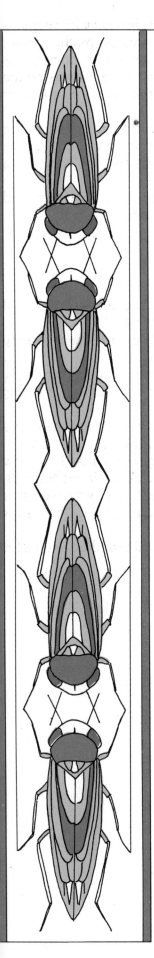

TABLE OF CONTENTS

1. WHAT MAKES AN INSECT
   AN INSECT? 4
   Describes how insects are classified, how insects
   are different from other animals, and the main
   characteristics of the insect group.

   ACTIVITIES 6
   • Insect Dance-Along
   • Little Kids' Scavenger Hunt
   • Tuned-In Tots
   • Build a Grasshopper
   • Mystery Creatures
   • Observe an Insect
   • Eight Legs or Six?
   • Insect Tree

   COPYCAT PAGES 13
   • Build a Grasshopper
   • Circle the Insect
   • Observe an Insect
   • Insect Picture Pages

2. GROWING UP 18
   Explains metamorphosis—the life stages that
   insects pass through.

   ACTIVITIES 19
   • Caterpillar Finger Play
   • There's a Beetle in My Flour
   • Caterpillar Capers
   • A Bucketful of Mosquitoes

   COPYCAT PAGES 23
   • Caterpillar Caper Maze
   • Insect Match-Up
   • Growing-Up Word Search

3. FINDING A PLACE
   TO LIVE 26
   Focuses on insect habitats and microhabitats—
   what they are and why they are so important to
   insects and all animals.

   ACTIVITIES 28
   • Amazing Insect Mouths
   • Insect Bingo
   • Who Lives Here?
   • Invent an Insect
   • Dipping for Aquatic Insects
   • Getting into Galls

   COPYCAT PAGES 32
   • Insect Bingo
   • Who Lives Here?
   • Amazing Insect Mouths

4. STAYING ALIVE 35
   Looks at how insects are adapted to survive.

   ACTIVITIES 37
   • Six-Legged Relay Race
   • Watch for Walking Sticks
   • Ant Detective
   • Population Count

   COPYCAT PAGES 42
   • An Ant's A-mazing World
   • The Hungry Bird
   • Ant Detective Worksheet

5. PEOPLE AND INSECTS 45
   Examines how insects influence our lives.

   ACTIVITIES 47
   • I Like Insects Because . . .
   • A Taste of Honey
   • Take a Trip
   • Insects on Stage
   • Insect Time Machine
   • Grasshopper Goulash and Maggot Muffins
   • Insects in the News

   COPYCAT PAGE 54
   • Insect Trivia

6. CRAFTY CORNER 55
   Provides activity ideas for using insects in art and
   craft projects.

   • Punched-Out Insects
   • Sculpting with Scraps
   • Marvelous Insect Model
   • Kooky Caterpillars
   • Insect Sculptures

7. APPENDIX . . : 58
   Provides instructions for building nets, traps, and
   cages; contains bibliography.

   • Traps, Nets, and Cages
   • Questions, Questions, and More Questions
   • Insect Glossary

1998 UPDATE

   TABLE OF CONTENTS 62
   WHAT INSECT IS IT? 63
   BUG-EYED 66
   WHAT A WAY TO GROW 69
   MOVE IT! 71
   SCARE TACTICS 72
   LAND OF THE GIANT INSECTS 73
   LAND AND WATER INSECTS 75
   COPYCAT PAGES 76
   INSECTS BIBLIOGRAPHY 92
   ANSWERS TO COPYCAT PAGES 94

WHAT MAKES AN INSECT AN INSECT?

All animals are classified according to how they look, how they behave, and how their bodies work in comparison with other animals' bodies. Animals with the same characteristics are grouped together.

Insects belong to the large group (phylum) of animals called *arthropods*. Arthropods include crayfish, spiders, millipedes, centipedes, ticks, mites, and similar creatures. Arthropods have jointed legs (in fact, the word *arthropod* means "jointed leg") and bodies that are divided into segments. (The segments are easy to see on millipedes or centipedes, but hard to see on some of the insects.) Insects are one group (class) of arthropods.

Here are some of the characteristics that are common to all insects:

Small size: Most insects are very small compared to birds, mammals, reptiles, and fish. Because of their small size they can live in places many other animals can't. Insects range in length from about 1/100th of an inch (.025 cm) to over 13 inches (32.5 cm).

Exoskeleton: Insects do not have skeletons inside their bodies for support as *vertebrates* (birds, mammals, reptiles, amphibians, and fish) do. Instead, they have a hard outer covering called an *exoskeleton*. (All arthropods, including spiders, mites, millipedes, and crayfish, have an exoskeleton.) It helps protect their internal organs and also helps prevent their drying out. The exoskeleton is made up of layers. The outside layer is waxy and acts like a waterproof raincoat. Underneath the waxy layer is a very tough, armor-like layer. The exoskeleton also acts as an anchor for insects' muscles.

Segments: All insects are made up of segments. Some segments overlap and allow the insects to be flexible. Insects have three main body parts—the *head,* the *thorax,* and the *abdomen.* With some insects it is almost impossible to see exactly where one main part starts and the next one stops. But here's an easy way to tell which part is which. Look for the *eyes, antennae,* and mouth on the *head.* The legs and wings are attached to the *thorax.* And the *abdomen* is what's left. (The head, thorax, and abdomen are further divided into smaller segments.)

Legs: Most insects have six legs. (A few have no legs at all.) By looking at an insect's legs, you can sometimes tell where an insect lives or what it eats. For example, mole crickets have digging legs with sharp claws and strong muscles in the front part of the leg. This allows them to tunnel quickly through soil. Many insects that live in water, such as water boatmen, have flattened, oar-like legs to help them paddle. Other insects, such as praying mantids and ambush bugs, have grasping legs. These insects use their grasping legs to capture their prey and hold on tight. Grasshoppers and fleas have jumping legs.

Wings: Insects are the only *invertebrates* (animals without backbones) that can fly. Only adult insects have wings. Being able to fly is a great advantage for insects. It means they can cover large distances to find new places to live, discover new food sources, escape quickly from enemies, and find mates. Some insects such as springtails, silverfish, bristletails, and ants, do not have wings; but most insects have two pairs. (Flies are the exception with only one pair of wings.) One way insects are identified and grouped into smaller subdivisions (orders) is by the arrangement of the veins in the wing.

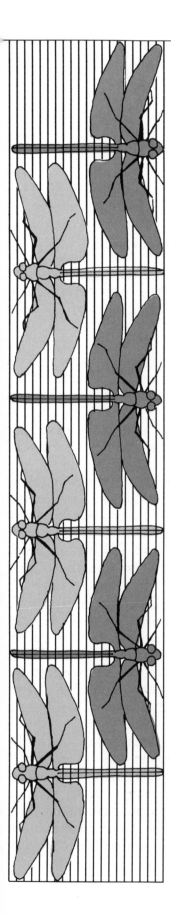

Eyes: Most insects have two types of eyes: simple and compound. The *compound eyes* are usually the biggest pair, often covering a large part of the head, although in some insects, especially those that live on the ground and eat plants, they are fairly small. The compound eyes are made up of thousands of tiny lenses that fit closely together. The lenses force light rays to bend and focus on special cells behind the eye. Each lens forms one little picture, and all the lenses together form a mosaic composite of the world around the insect.

This mosaic picture is not very sharp and lacks detail. Compared to people, most insects have poor eyesight. For example, a person can see 100 times more detail than a honey bee. However, the more lenses in the compound eye the better the insect can see. Dragonflies have the best eyesight, some having over 25,000 separate lenses in each eye. House flies have over 4,000. Compound eyes can recognize color and pattern and are very sensitive to movement. Usually only adults and nymphs have compound eyes.

Many insects also have a triangle of three *simple eyes* between their compound eyes, although some have only two, one, or none. Most *entomologists* (scientists who study insects) are not sure exactly how these simple eyes are used, but they know the eyes are sensitive to light and dark.

Antennae: Most insects have a pair of sensitive antennae on their heads. These are used to feel, smell, and, in some insects, hear. Insect antennae differ in size, shape, and how they are used. You can frequently tell which insect is which just by looking at its antennae. With certain insects, such as moths and mosquitoes, you can often tell the males from the females by comparing the antennae. (The males' antennae are more feathery than the females'. The males use their antennae to pick up the scent of a potential mate. See discussion of pheromones below.)

Hairs: Insects are covered with thousands of sensory hairs that stick out of their exoskeletons. The hairs are connected to the central nervous system and are very sensitive to movement, pressure, smell, and sound. Thousands of hairs cover the legs, antennae, and all other body parts of insects.

Insect Blood: Insects have a very simple circulatory system. They do not have a complex network of veins and arteries, as more advanced animals do. Instead they have a simple heart that pumps blood through open body cavities. The blood is almost colorless and does not carry oxygen. (Vertebrate blood contains hemoglobin, an iron compound that carries oxygen to the cells. Hemoglobin is what makes vertebrate blood red.) Insect blood carries dissolved food to the cells and carries off waste materials.

Pheromones: Many insects can produce chemicals, called *pheromones,* that communicate messages to other insects. One function of insect pheromones is to attract the opposite sex. The strength of these chemical attractants can be amazing. Female silkworm moths, for example, can produce pheromones that male silkworm moths can detect up to two miles away!

Besides being powerful sex attractants, pheromones serve other purposes. Ants that find a good food source may produce a "pheromone trail" when they return to their ant hill with some of the food. Then other ants can follow the trail back to the food source without getting lost.

Insect pheromones are used to help control insect pests. For more about this human use of pheromones, see page 46 of the "People and Insects" section.

Insect Dance-Along

Move like insects and dance to insect songs.

Objectives:
Describe how different kinds of insects move in different ways. Demonstrate insect movements through song and dance.

Ages:
Primary

Materials:
- *pictures of insects (see activity for suggestions)*

Subjects:
Physical Education and Science

Here's an active way for children to learn about some common insects and how they move. Have them sing and dance along with each verse of the insect songs that follow. Show them pictures of each insect before you begin. Also practice crawling, hopping, flying, swimming, and digging.

To the tune of "Frere Jacques":
- Crawling beetle, crawling beetle,
  On the ground, on the ground,
  Crawling, crawling, crawling,
  Crawling, crawling, crawling,
  All around, all around.

- Hopping cricket,
  Hopping cricket,
  In the grass, in the grass,
  Hopping, hopping, hopping,
  Hopping, hopping, hopping,
  Very fast, very fast.

- Busy bumble bee, busy bumble bee,
  In the air, in the air,
  Flying, flying, flying,
  Flying, flying, flying,
  Buzzing here, buzzing there.

Other ideas: Swimming backswimmer, digging mole cricket

To the tune of "You Are My Sunshine":
- I am a cricket,
  A big black cricket,
  I have 6 legs and 2 pairs of wings.
  My body's covered
  With an exoskeleton,
  And I rub my wings to sing.

Little Kids' Scavenger Hunt

Make collecting containers and search for insect clues.

Objective:
Describe what some insects eat and where they live.

Ages:
Primary

Materials:
- *small (8 oz.) milk cartons*
- *string*
- *paper*
- *glue*
- *pictures of insects (optional)*

Subject:
Science

Go outside with your kids and have them find:
- something an insect eats
- something an insect could live in or on
- something the color of a grasshopper
- something an insect has nibbled on

When the scavenger hunt is finished have everyone sit in a circle and show what was found for each "something."

Here's how to make a collecting container to use on the scavenger hunt:

Take a small milk carton and open the top all the way. Rinse it out, poke a hole in either side of the carton below the top folds (so it'll still be able to close), and tie a string through the holes and across the top for a handle.

Have the kids paste pictures of insects on three sides and a plain piece of paper (for their names) on the fourth.

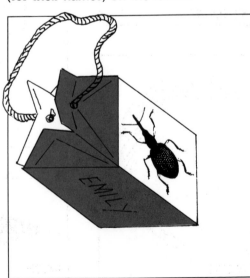

Tuned-In Tots

Make and wear insect antennae using pipe cleaners and foil.

Objectives:
Compare insect senses with those people have. Describe how an animal's senses are important to it.

Ages:
Primary

Materials:
- *aluminum foil*
- *insect pictures*
- *pipe cleaners*
- *beads*
- *Styrofoam balls (optional)*
- *pictures of insects*

Subject:
Science

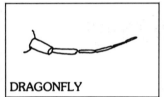

DRAGONFLY

MOSQUITO

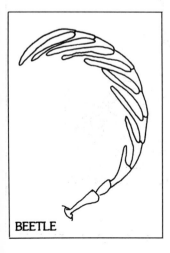

BEETLE

Like people, insects sense what's around them by touching, smelling, tasting, seeing, and hearing. Each type of insect uses a combination of different sense organs. Antennae are very important sense organs for insects. Insects use their antennae for feeling, smelling, tasting, and sometimes hearing what's around them. Many insects also have very sensitive body hairs, which can pick up smells and vibrations in the air. Some insects have taste receptors on their feet. Many hear with special ear drums on their abdomen or legs. And most see with compound and/or simple eyes.

Have your kids make their own antennae to better understand how insects use theirs to sense what's around them. Start by showing pictures of common insects that have different-shaped antennae. (For example, dragonfly antennae are short and bristle-like, some beetle antennae are short and club-like, termite antennae are bead-like, and butterfly antennae are long with knobs on their ends.) Point to other antennae and talk about the different ways antennae are used. (Male moth antennae pick up chemical scents in the air released by the female; male mosquito antennae pick up vibrations from the female.)

Your kids can use either aluminum foil and pipe cleaners or just plain aluminum foil to make their antennae. For the all-foil antennae, give each child two long (3 x 12")

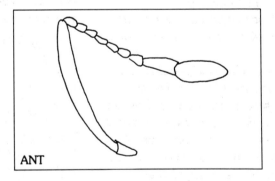

ANT

MOTH

and two shorter (3 x 10") pieces of aluminum foil. Have the kids roll and twist the longer pieces into a headband. Then have them roll and twist the two shorter pieces into antennae, leaving the ends flat. Wrap the flat ends around the headband.

Another option is to curl pipe cleaners (instead of foil) around the foil headbands. This way the kids can choose their own antennae colors. Plus, pipe cleaner antennae are great for "segmenting": just have the kids stack tiny wooden or plastic beads onto each pipe cleaner after they've attached it to the headband. Or they can attach a single bead or Styrofoam ball on the end of each antenna.

When the kids finish, have them wear their antennae while you discuss senses. Here are some questions to ask your antennaed kids:

- What are our five senses? (taste, sight, touch, smell, and hearing)
- What parts of our body do we use for these senses?
- Do insects have the same senses? (Yes, but insects and people use their senses in different ways and have different abilities. For example, insects cannot see as clearly as people can, but some can see ultraviolet light, which we can't see.)
- What would it be like to have antennae? (How would we greet people, smell dinner cooking, and get around in a dark room?)
- What would happen if you were an insect and you injured or broke off your antennae? (You probably wouldn't survive. You'd need antennae to find food, escape from enemies, and find a mate.)

Build a Grasshopper

Put together a grasshopper puzzle and label its parts.

Objectives:
Construct a model of a grasshopper and label the body parts. List three characteristics of an insect.

Ages:
Primary and Intermediate

Materials:
- *copies of page 13*
- *pencils and crayons*
- *construction paper*
- *rulers*   • *glue*

Subject: *Science*

This "parts chart" activity is a good way to introduce or review the parts of an insect. First give each person a copy of the grasshopper squares on page 13. Have the group follow the directions for building a grasshopper by cutting out all of the squares, pasting them in place on another sheet of paper, and labeling the parts according to the sample on their Copycat Page. For a neater chart, have them use a ruler when labeling.

LIVE HOPPERS

Before or after you do this activity, it would be great if the group could watch a live grasshopper in action. They'd get a chance to see how the legs work, how the wings fold back over the abdomen, how the compound eyes look close up, where the mouth is, and how the grasshopper breathes. (Check the Appendix for ways to catch insects. And be sure to release the grasshopper where it was found.)

Mystery Creatures

Listen to an insect story and try to draw the mystery creature described.

Objectives:
Describe several insect characteristics. Practice creative drawing and listening skills.

Ages:
Primary, Intermediate, and Advanced

Materials:
- *colored pencils or crayons*
- *paper*
- *pictures of an assassin bug or a monarch butterfly*

Subjects:
Science and Art

One way for children to learn about insect characteristics is for them to draw an insect. Use these mystery creature stories to get your group thinking about what insects look like. (Use the monarch butterfly story for younger children and the assassin bug story for more advanced children.)

Read the description and tell the kids to listen carefully as you read. Tell them to try to form a picture in their minds of what is being described. Suggest that they take notes on any body characteristics they hear described.

After reading the description to them, have each person draw a picture of the creature they've imagined. Tell them to include as many details as they can remember.

Afterward, show them a picture of the real thing. (In the first story it's an assassin bug. And in the second story, it's a monarch butterfly. Look in Simon and Schuster's *Guide to Insects* by Dr. Ross Arnett: page 53 for assassin bug; page 239 for monarch butterfly.) Discuss the insect characteristics that were described in the story. You can do this activity with any creature and add more description and a longer text for more advanced students.

SILENT STALKER

The creature crawled slowly through the field. Its long jointed legs were colored with bands of black and white. Tiny claws on the end of each leg grasped the stalks of grasses and weeds tightly as it moved along.

The creature had one giant bulging eye on each side of its cone-like head. The eyes seemed odd and unnatural . . . made up of hundreds of tiny lenses.

The creature moved stiffly, its hard armor shielding it from springing stems of grass and weeds. As it moved, two long stalks on top of its head swayed from side to side and up and down. Just like its legs, the stalks were ringed with black and white.

Suddenly the creature halted, motionless except for the two stalks moving ever so slightly as they tested the air. One moment . . . two . . . then POUNCE! The creature reached out and grabbed its prey, piercing the smaller creature's smooth armor with a long sucking tube. As if using a straw, the larger creature drained the juices from the body of its prey.

When the creature was no longer hungry, it left the carcass lying in the dew-soaked field and clambered away through the tangled weeds.

The black-and-white legged stalker was not a large creature—perhaps an inch (2.5 cm) long. But its body was bizarre. There were three parts, all encased in a thin coat of armor. The cone-like head was followed by a flattened, triangular back, and wings folded over the rest of its body. The armor was brown with orange markings. Hairs and short bristles stuck up from its head and legs.

Again the creature stopped. Since it was not feeding, its long sucking tube lay folded under its chin and body. The field was almost silent, except for an occasional rustle in the weeds. It was time for the creature to rest.

WINGS OF ORANGE AND BLACK

Jeffrey sat on the edge of his porch. He was bored. Nothing exciting had happened all day. Suddenly a bright, colorful creature appeared in front of him. It flew past the porch and disappeared around the corner of the house.

Jeffrey jumped up and ran to the side of the house. The creature was perched on top of a big yellow flower. Its four wings, shaped like triangles, were bright orange with black along the edges. Its body was narrow and black and had six long legs.

A breeze gently rocked the creature but it held on tightly. It bent its head down, uncoiled its long tongue, and stuck it into the center of the flower. Sweet, sugary nectar flowed into its mouth.

Jeffrey wanted to get a close look. It would be great to tell his family all about the creature. He took one step and then another. Whoosh . . . the creature took off. It slowly flapped its orange and black wings and landed on another flower farther away.

Quietly Jeffrey tiptoed toward the creature. As he got closer and closer he could see the creature's head. Two big black eyes stared at him. Swaying back and forth on top of the creature's head were two long stalks with knobs on the ends. Then whoosh . . . the creature took off again. This time it flew over the fence and disappeared. Jeffrey smiled and waved. The creature had brightened his day.

Observe an Insect

Collect insects and observe them up close.

Objectives:
Describe the characteristics of an insect. Identify places to look for insects.

Ages:
Intermediate and Advanced

Materials:
- *plastic containers or Ziploc bags*
- *pencils*
- *insect field guides*
- *hand lenses (optional)*
- *copies of page 15*
- *insect nets (optional)*

Subject:
Science

One of the best things about studying insects is that you can find them almost everywhere. But once you find one, how can you tell what kind it is? The only way is to look at its many different characteristics.

The insect *class* is divided into smaller groups called *orders* based on characteristics such as:
- type of mouthparts (sucking, lapping, chewing, etc.)
- number of veins in the wings
- types of legs (grasping, digging, swimming, hopping, etc.)
- behavior
- wing shape

There are about 26 insect orders. Not all entomologists agree on exactly how many orders there are. Some lump certain orders together, and others split certain orders into two or three. Each order has a Latinized name that describes a major characteristic of it. For example, moths and butterflies belong to the order *Lepidoptera,* which means "scaly wings." Flies belong to the order *Diptera,* which means "two wings."

In this activity your kids will go on an insect search, capture a live insect, and then observe it closely to describe its characteristics and see which order it belongs to.

Before you go on the search, scout out a nearby area, looking for a place that has a lot of good insect habitats. Weedy patches, damp forest soil, rotting logs, pond edges, stream banks, and gardens are great places to look. Some good insects to study are crickets, grasshoppers, praying mantids, beetles, ants, termites, butterfly and moth larvae (caterpillars), cockroaches, caddisfly larvae, and cicadas. (*Avoid* stinging and biting insects such as bees, wasps, and assassin bugs. Also watch out for poison ivy and poison oak.)

Give each person a plastic container. Tell your kids to spread out and try to find one insect for each container. Explain that all the insects will be released after the activity so they should place them gently into the containers. (It is very easy to

damage a wing or a leg.) To catch flying insects, such as moths, butterflies, and flies, you might want the group to make nets. See page 58 in the Appendix.

Once everyone has caught an insect, head back inside to conduct your studies. Give each person a copy of the worksheet and have them each answer the questions. Pass out hand lenses so that the kids can really get a close-up look.

Once the worksheets are completed, have the kids use field guides to try to find out what kinds of insects they have. Then go around the room and have each person tell the group something interesting about his or her insect. Survey the group and find out:
- What was the hardest question to answer? Why?
- How many found they didn't really have an insect? What did they have? (maybe a spider, centipede, millipede, snail, sowbug, or earthworm)
- Who had the largest insects? The smallest?
- What special adaptations did each insect have? (pincers, special odor, large compound eyes, jumping legs, etc.)

As a follow-up, have the kids compare insects with other types of animals. This will give them a better understanding of how other animals are grouped and the characteristics insects share with them. (You can either use pictures or bring in live animals to use for comparison.) For example, hold up a picture of a turtle and have the kids find four similarities and four differences between insects and turtles. (See lists on top of next page.)

Afterward, take a walk to release all the insects where you found them.

SIMILARITIES

Both insects and turtles:

- have mouths
- live in forests, ponds, or fields
- have eyes
- have hard outer coverings (turtles—shell, insects—exoskeleton)
- breathe air

DIFFERENCES

INSECTS	TURTLES
• 6 legs	• 4 legs
• wings	• no wings
• antennae	• no antennae
• take in air through spiracles (tiny holes on their sides)	• take in air through the nostrils
• compound eyes	• simple eyes

Eight Legs or Six?

Divide into insect and spider teams and make picture postcards to send to the other team.

Objective:
Compare body structure, life histories, and habitats of insects and spiders.

Ages:
Intermediate and Advanced

Materials:
- *large pictures of spiders and insects*
- *cardboard or blank index cards*
- *paper bags*
- *markers or colored pencils*
- *names of insects and spiders on slips of paper*

Subjects:
Science and Creative Writing

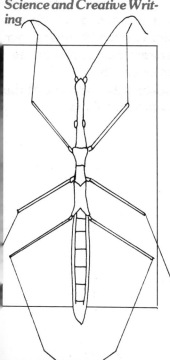

 Insects and spiders are very closely related and people often confuse the two. But you can tell them apart by looking at several different characteristics and watching how the animals live. Listed below are some general differences between spiders and insects.

INSECTS
- usually have 6 legs
- have 3 main body parts (head, thorax, and abdomen)

- found in water and on land
- have antennae
- eat a variety of things, from plants to animals to decayed material
- most don't spin silk, and those that do usually spin it from glands in their mouths
- usually have 2 compound eyes and several simple eyes
- usually have two pairs of wings

SPIDERS
- have 8 legs

- have 2 main body parts (cephalothorax, which is the head and thorax fused together, and abdomen)
- usually live on land
- have no antennae
- usually are carnivorous and paralyze their prey with poison

- most spin silk from spinnerets on their abdomens

- usually have 8 simple eyes and no compound eyes

- have no wings

Here's an activity that emphasizes the differences and similarities between spiders and insects.

PICTURE POSTCARDS

Cut out pictures of spiders and insects and hang them around the room. (You can also bring in live insects and spiders in glass jars so kids can watch these animals close up.) Write the names of different kinds of insects and spiders on separate slips of paper so that there are enough for each person. (Make an equal number of spider and insect slips.)

As a group, discuss the differences between spiders and insects. Point out the differences and similarities and make a list on the board or on a flip chart. Then divide the group into "spiders" and "insects" by having each person pick a slip of paper. Pair up a spider and an insect and pass out a piece of fairly stiff cardboard (4¼ x 5½") or a large, blank index card to each person.

Tell them that each has to send a picture postcard to his or her partner. Here's how they'll do it:

- Go to the library in small groups to find out about their animals (what they look like, where they live, and what they eat).

- Draw a picture of their insect or spider on one side of the postcard.
- On the other side, address the postcard to the habitat where the other person's animal might live. (for example, praying mantid—field; fishing spider—edge of pond)

- In the remaining space on the address side, write something about what their creature does and how it is the same as or different from their partners'. For example, here's what a praying mantid might write to a garden spider:

Dear Gerry Garden Spider,
Today I was crawling in the garden and saw a huge beetle. I grabbed it with my grasping front legs. It was probably something you would have liked too.
Sincerely,
Paula Praying Mantid

By putting themselves in the place of a spider or insect, the kids will get a better feel for what each type of creature looks like and needs to stay alive. Afterward, have the kids exchange postcards. Then sit in a circle and have them read their partners' postcards aloud to the other kids. Have them look at the pictures of insects and spiders that are hanging around the room as the postcards are read. Here are some good insects and spiders to use:

- *Insects:* grasshopper, termite, praying mantid, dragonfly, ant, wasp, bee, butterfly, moth, cockroach, cicada.
- *Spiders:* garden spider, jumping spider, house spider, black widow, tarantula, trapdoor spider, fishing spider, crab spider, wolf spider, lynx spider.

Insect Tree

Cut out insect pictures to color and decorate.

Objectives:
Describe insect shapes and colors. Use a field guide.

Ages:
Intermediate

Materials:
- *copies of pages 16 and 17*
- *crayons, markers, or colored pencils*
- *construction paper*
- *hole puncher*
- *glue*
- *yarn*
- *clay*

Subjects:
Science and Art

H ere's a great way to make an "indoor" insect collection. Give each person a copy of the insect picture pages (on pages 16 and 17). Have them color the insects with crayons, colored pencils, or markers. To find out what colors to make the insects have the kids look up each insect in a field guide. (See bibliography for a list of common guides.)

After the insects are colored, have the kids paste the page to a sheet of colored construction paper. Then have them cut out each insect and its name as shown, and punch a hole in each cut-out.

Have each person collect a small dead tree branch and place the base of the branch into a piece of soft clay. To finish their insect trees, have them tie each insect to a different twig with yarn.

If you would like to have one tree for the whole group you can bring in a large branch and give each child one insect to look up, color, and attach to the tree.

BUILD A GRASSHOPPER

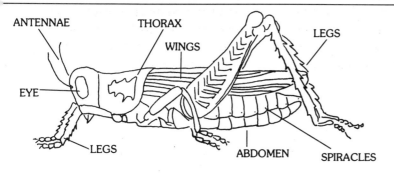

Turn this mixed-up insect into a grasshopper! Cut out the pieces along the dotted lines and glue them together to make a grasshopper. Then label these parts: HEAD, THORAX, ABDOMEN, EYE, ANTENNAE, LEGS, WINGS, and SPIRACLES. Here's what it should look like when you're done.

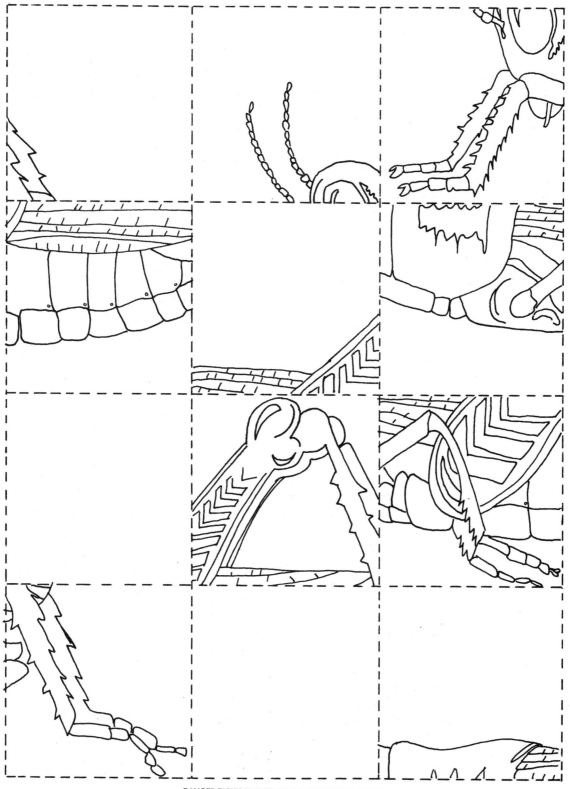

13

How many of these animals are insects? See how many you can find and circle.

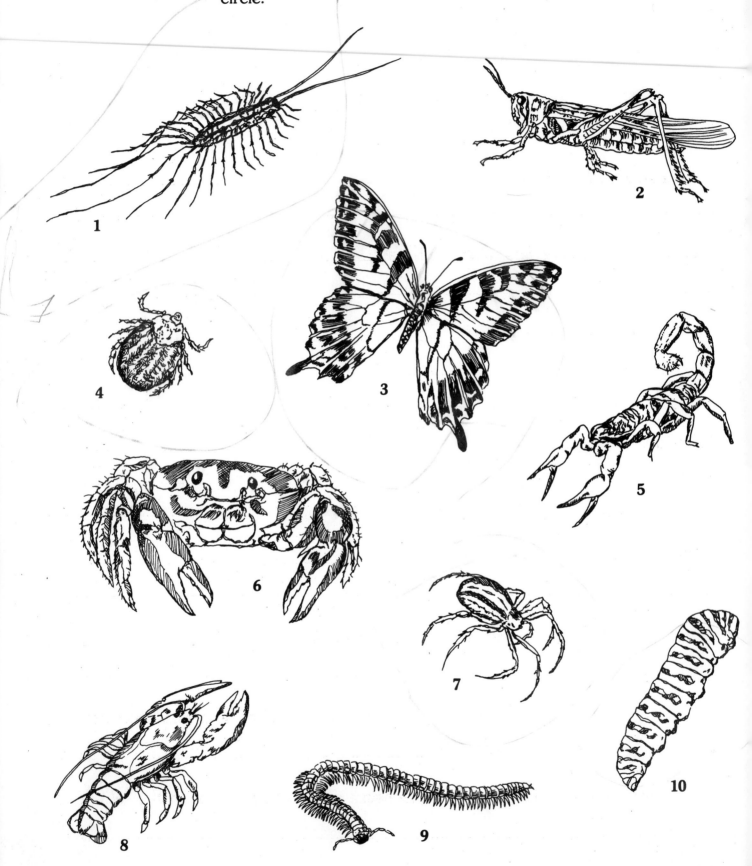

1

2

3

4

5

6

7

8

9

10

RANGER RICK'S NATURESCOPE: INCREDIBLE INSECTS

1. Draw a picture of your insect.

2. Describe where you found it. _____

_____

3. What kind of insect do you think you have? _____

_____

4. Why do you think it's an insect? _____

_____

_____

5. How does it move? _____

_____

_____

6. What do you think your insect eats? _____

_____

7. Make up a name for your insect based on how it looks. _____

_____

8. Watch your insect for a few minutes. Make up a name for it based on how it behaves. _____

9. Name three things about your insect that help it to live where you found it. _____

_____

_____

INSECT PICTURE PAGES

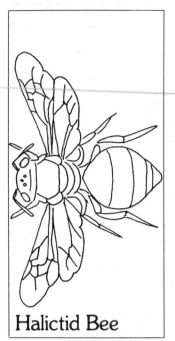

Halictid Bee

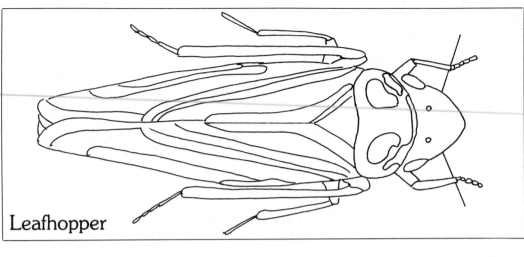

Leafhopper

House Fly

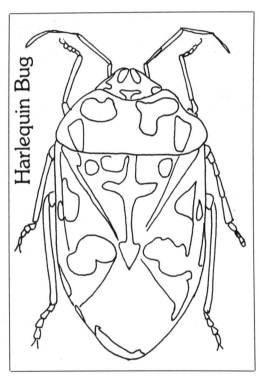

Harlequin Bug

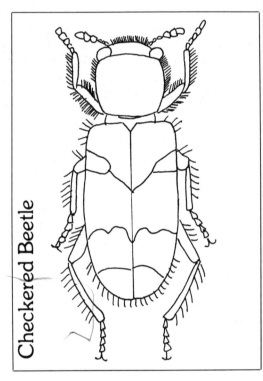

Checkered Beetle

Grasshopper

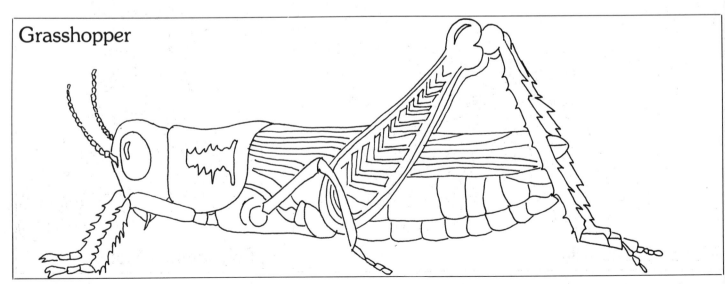

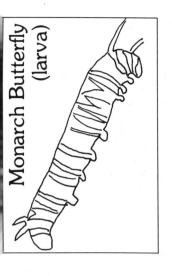

Monarch Butterfly (larva)

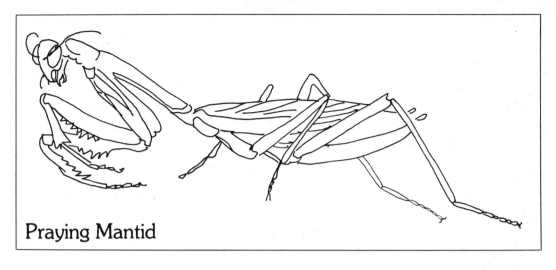

Praying Mantid

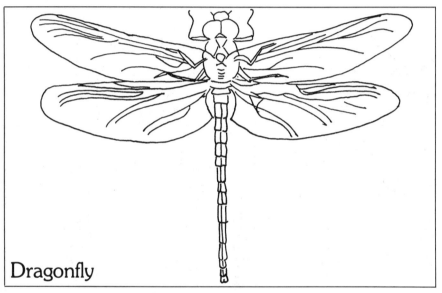

Dragonfly

Honey Bee

Monarch Butterfly

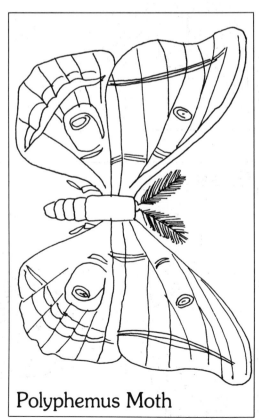

Polyphemus Moth

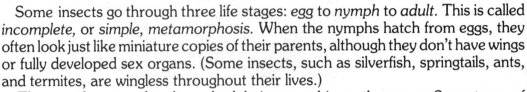

GROWING UP

ost insects hatch from eggs and go through several stages of life. The process of changing from egg to adult is called *metamorphosis.* (Metamorphosis means "to change.") The activities in this section focus on insect life cycles and how insects change from egg to adult.

Some insects go through three life stages: *egg* to *nymph* to *adult.* This is called *incomplete,* or *simple, metamorphosis.* When the nymphs hatch from eggs, they often look just like miniature copies of their parents, although they don't have wings or fully developed sex organs. (Some insects, such as silverfish, springtails, ants, and termites, are wingless throughout their lives.)

The nymphs eat and *molt,* or shed their outer skin, as they grow. Some types of insect nymphs molt only a few times before they become adults; others molt many times. Finally, on the last molt, the wings and sex organs have developed and the insect emerges as an adult.

The nymphs of some insects that go through incomplete metamorphosis live in the water and do not resemble the adults. (These nymphs are often called *naiads.*) Dragonflies, mayflies, and stoneflies are examples.

More advanced insects go through four life stages: *egg* to *larva* to *pupa* to *adult.* This is called *complete metamorphosis.* The young of these insects are called *larvae* (singular is larva). With these insects, the larvae do not look like the adults. For example, a caterpillar is the larval stage of a butterfly. Larvae and adults look very different from one another and eat different foods. During complete metamorphosis the larva will change into a pupa, or resting stage, after its last molt. During the pupal stage the insect slowly goes through many chemical changes that rearrange its whole body structure. When it emerges from the pupal stage, it will be an adult.

Insects that go through incomplete metamorphosis: springtails, silverfish, dragonflies, mayflies, termites, stoneflies, crickets, grasshoppers, mantids, earwigs, cockroaches, lice, true bugs, aphids, cicadas, and thrips.

Insects that go through complete metamorphosis: lacewings, antlions, butterflies, moths, flies, fleas, ants, bees, wasps, and beetles.

Caterpillar Finger Play

Imitate the changes from caterpillar to butterfly with finger movements.

Objective:
Demonstrate the life cycle of a butterfly with fingers and hands.

Ages:
Primary

Materials:
- *pictures of butterflies at each stage of life*

Subject:
Science

Photos by Maurice LeFranc

Begin this activity by describing the life cycle of the butterfly. (See background material on page 18.) Show the children pictures of the butterfly eggs, and the caterpillar, chrysalis, and adult stages.

Have the kids start the finger play with their arms at their sides.

WORDS	ACTION
Ten little eggs,	Hold hands up, fingers straight.
All in a mound.	Join hands together in a ball.
Out come caterpillars, Crawling all around.	Extend and wiggle fingers.
Next they will sleep And we know why.	Lay head to one side on hands.
Soon they'll come out as butterflies.	Hold hands up, fingers straight. Wave fingers.

There's a Beetle in My Flour

Describe the changes that take place in a mealworm colony.

Objectives:
Define complete metamorphosis. Describe each stage in the life cycle of a darkling beetle.

Ages:
Primary and Intermediate

Materials:
- *mealworms (available at most pet stores)*
- *large jar*
- *oatmeal or bran*
- *small piece of screening*
- *rubber band*
- *apple or potato*
- *food for adult darkling beetles (see activity for suggestions)*
- *dissecting microscope (optional)*

Subjects:
Science and Math

Have you ever opened a bag of flour or dog food and noticed black or brown beetles crawling around? Those beetles were probably darkling beetles. There are many different kinds of darkling beetles. Some, called flour beetles, feed on flour, corn meal, dog food, cereal, dried fruit, and all kinds of stored grain. These beetles are serious pests in grocery stores and warehouses.

The larvae of some darkling beetles are called mealworms. (The larvae of many other beetles are called grubs.) Mealworms are often sold in pet stores as food for lizards, snakes, turtles, and other pets. You can purchase a small container of mealworms and raise your own beetle colony. That way, your kids can watch firsthand how beetles change from eggs to adults.

First fill a large jar with oatmeal or bran. Add a wedge of apple or potato to provide moisture for the mealworms. (By nibbling at the apple or potato, they will get all the water they need.) Place the mealworms in the jar and cover the top with a small piece of screening. Fasten with a rubber band.

Check the jar every few days to make sure it is moist, but not too wet. Mealworms remain as larvae for up to four months. Since you probably won't know how old they were when you purchased them, watch them daily.

The kids can observe the entire life cycle in the jar of cereal. The mealworm larvae will change into stiff, white pupae. Then in a short while the pupae will change into beetles. Feed the beetles small bits of raw vegetables (such as carrots and turnips), cornmeal, and dog food. The adults will lay eggs that are very tiny, clear white, and sticky. The eggs will hatch within 5 to 12 days, starting a new generation of mealworms.

MEALWORM ACTIVITIES

- Think of ways to find out how mealworms react to temperature changes. How are the eggs affected by temperature changes?

- What is the average length of a mealworm?

- Grow two or three separate colonies and feed each one something different (oatmeal, bran, dog food). Is there a difference in size? color? behavior? rate of development?

- Have the kids keep "beetle books" and illustrate each stage in the beetle's life cycle.

- Under a dissecting microscope look at the beetle's antennae, compound eyes, legs, and hard outer wings. Have the kids sketch each body part in their notebooks.

- Have the kids write a story about a day in the life of a mealworm or flour beetle.

- Take a walk with your group to look for beetle grubs, pupae, and adults. For grubs and pupae, search inside rotting logs and stumps or in the soil. For adults, look on flowerheads, garden plants, and trees and shrubs.

For more mealworm activities, see SCIS (Science Curriculum Improvement Study) units on environments and organisms. Write to: Delta Education, P.O. Box M, Nashua, NH 03061-6012.

BRANCHING OUT: MATH

After studying about mealworms and beetle life cycles, try making up some mealworm math problems for your group. Adapt these ideas to fit your needs:

Fractions
If a female darkling beetle laid 92 eggs and each egg hatched, but only half of them lived to be adults, how many adult beetles would there be?
$(92 \div 2 = 46)$

Averaging
If there are 4032 beetles living in your backyard, 5672 beetles living in your neighbor's yard, and 7921 beetles living in my backyard, what is the average number of beetles per yard?
$(4032 + 7921 + 5672) \div 3 = 5875$

Caterpillar Capers

Rear caterpillars and watch them change into butterflies and moths.

Objectives:
Describe the life cycle of a butterfly. Design and maintain an insect habitat.

Ages:
All

Materials:
- *gallon jar or small aquarium*
- *screened lid*
- *fresh leaves daily*
- *twigs and soil*
- *caterpillar*

Subject:
Science

The most exciting way to learn about metamorphosis is to watch an insect as it develops. Some of the easiest insects for kids to find are caterpillars—the larvae of moths and butterflies.

To raise a caterpillar indoors, your group will need to make a home for it in a gallon jar or small aquarium. Fill the bottom of the cage with soil and add a few twigs. Then cover the cage with a screened lid for good ventilation.

Growing caterpillars need a lot of food—fresh green leaves every day. But caterpillars are often fussy, eating only certain kinds of leaves. When you capture your caterpillar be sure to identify the plant it was feeding on and give it only that type of leaf. (The kids can take turns bringing in caterpillar food.)

When it is time to *pupate* (spin a *cocoon* or form a *chrysalis*), some caterpillars will attach themselves to a twig and others will burrow into the soil. In areas of the country that have freezing temperatures in winter, the pupae that normally overwinter will need to be exposed to the cold. (The amount of time varies with the species.) So put your cage or jar outside. The cold triggers chemical reactions that cause the insects to change into adults. If you leave your cocoon or chrysalis outside, the adults will emerge when the temperature gets warmer. Some moths and butterflies crawl out in spring, others in summer and early fall.

When the moth or butterfly emerges, you can identify it and observe it for a day or two. Then let it go. It will probably mate and produce a new generation in the wild.

A Bucketful of Mosquitoes

Raise mosquitoes in a bucket and get a close-up look at their eggs, larvae, pupae, and adults.

Objectives:
Observe and record mosquito metamorphosis. Recognize that some insects have aquatic stages in their development.

Ages:
Intermediate and Advanced

Materials:
- *bucket or dishpan*
- *piece of burlap*
- *pond water*
- *strainer*
- *magnifying glass*
- *fertilizer or plant food*
- *window screening to cover the bucket*

Subjects:
Science and Language Arts

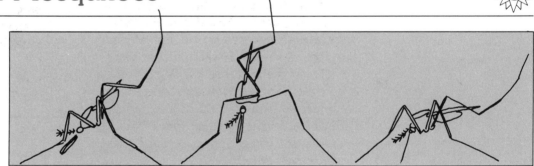

To watch how a fly develops from egg to adult (yes, a mosquito is a type of fly), make a mosquito breeding bucket. Your kids can watch as the eggs hatch into *wrigglers* (mosquito larvae), then change into *tumblers* (mosquito pupae), and finally fly away as adults. During this activity, have the kids keep mosquito notebooks to record all their observations, make sketches of what they observe, and write down any questions they may think of.

How to Do It:
Line a bucket or dishpan with burlap and fill it halfway with tap water. Let it stand outside for a day so that any chlorine in the water will disappear. Then add some filtered pond water. (Pour it through a strainer to keep out all the larger mosquito predators.)

Add a pinch of fertilizer or plant food to help speed the growth of algae in the water. The algae will provide food for the mosquito larvae. You can also sprinkle a pinch of ground-up dog biscuits on the surface of the water for larvae food.

Now wait and watch and hope that an adult female mosquito comes by and lays eggs on the water. One of the most common mosquitoes (*Culex*) lays its eggs in floating *rafts,* or clumps, on the surface. Other kinds of mosquitoes lay them singly or at the water's edge. Once you see the eggs, cover the container with a piece of

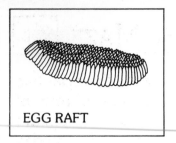

EGG RAFT

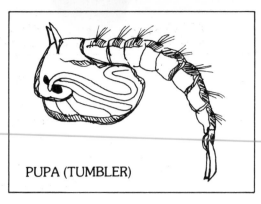

PUPA (TUMBLER)

LARVA
(WRIGGLER)

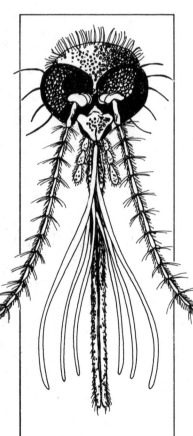

HEAD OF ADULT FEMALE

- How the adults crawl out of the pupal cases
- What time of day the mosquitoes are most active
- How many eggs are in a raft
- The size and shape of the antennae (on the males they are very bushy; the females have shorter, less feathery ones)
- What other creatures are in the water

window screening.

Each day have your kids examine the bucket with a magnifying glass and record everything they see. In one to five days the eggs should hatch into wrigglers. (For a good close-up picture of a mosquito larva, see *Ranger Rick*, May 1978, page 5.) The wrigglers will swim around for one to two weeks and then change into tumblers. Mosquito tumblers are unlike many other insect pupae because they move around. In a few days the adults will emerge.

If, despite your efforts, your container fails to attract mosquitoes, try finding some eggs, wrigglers, or tumblers that you can transfer to your bucket or dishpan. Almost any source of standing water is a good place to search: ponds, stagnant pools; even old tires with standing water inside make good mosquito breeding grounds.

Here are some things to have your kids look for as your mosquito "family" develops:

- **How the larvae breathe** (They hang upside down from the surface and breathe through a breathing tube on their abdomen.)
- **How the pupae breathe** (They breathe at the surface with a pair of breathing tubes on their thorax.)

After observing for a few days, add some *unfiltered* pond water to the bucket. Try to get as many pond predators as possible (dragonfly and damselfly nymphs, small fish, etc.). Also add some pond plants and bottom mud. Have the kids watch to see what eats the mosquito eggs, larvae, and pupae.

Talk about mosquito pest problems. (Many spread diseases to people and other animals, and they are difficult to control because they reproduce so quickly and are resistant to many types of chemical controls.) Then discuss how predators are now used to help control mosquitoes. (Dragonflies and fish are introduced into mosquito-infested areas.)

When your experiment is done, pour the water back into the pond and clean up the equipment. If you leave standing water outside, you will breed mosquitoes all season.

As a follow-up go on a mosquito patrol in your neighborhood. Look for mosquito breeding areas. How have people created mosquito breeding habitats (piles of old tires with standing water inside, polluted streams of stagnant water)? Plan a clean-up of your neighborhood to get rid of as many potential mosquito breeding sites as you can.

BRANCHING OUT: LANGUAGE ARTS

Make Up Mosquito Poems

After studying mosquitoes and other insect life cycles, have your group make up some humorous insect poems. One type to try is a limerick. Limericks are humorous poems written in a special meter with five lines. (For you poetry experts, the first, second, and fifth lines have 3 feet, and the third and fourth lines have 2 feet.) Lines 1, 2, and 5 rhyme with each other and lines 3 and 4 rhyme with each other. Here's an example:

There was a mosquito named Newman,
Who wanted some blood from a human.
  She sat on my hat
  And I squashed her flat,
Goodbye to her buzzin' and zoomin'.

COPYCAT PAGE

CATERPILLAR CAPER MAZE

Help this monarch caterpillar find its way to another clump of milkweed. Then draw a picture of what you think will someday crawl out of the chrysalis that is hanging from the milkweed plant.

RANGER RICK'S NATURESCOPE: INCREDIBLE INSECTS

ADULTS

Draw a line to connect each insect adult with the picture of its larva or nymph.

NYMPHS & LARVAE

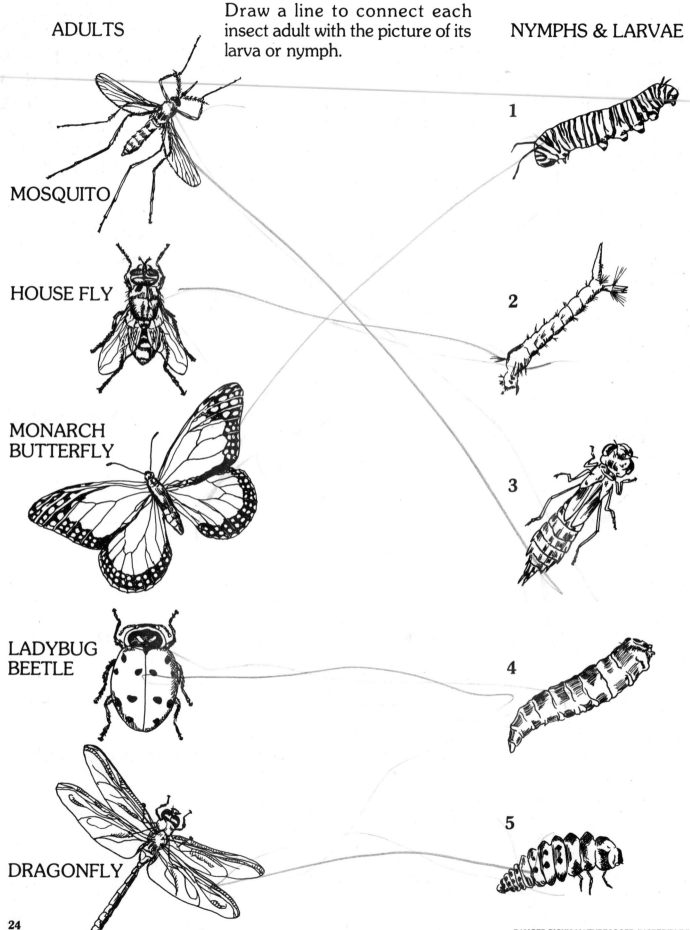

MOSQUITO

HOUSE FLY

MONARCH BUTTERFLY

LADYBUG BEETLE

DRAGONFLY

1

2

3

4

5

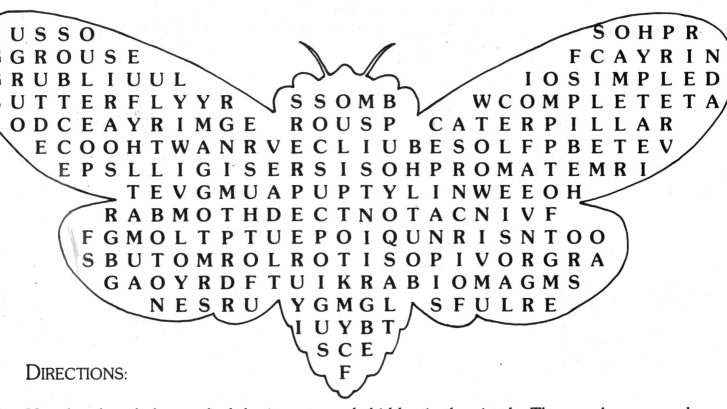

```
U S S O                                              S O H P R
G R O U S E                                        F C A Y R I N
R U B L I U U L                                  I O S I M P L E D
U T T E R F L Y Y R        S S O M B            W C O M P L E T E T A
O D C E A Y R I M G E    R O U S P    C A T E R P I L L A R
E C O O H T W A N R V E C L I U B E S O L F P B E T E V
E P S L L I G I S E R S I S O H P R O M A T E M R I
    T E V G M U A P U P T Y L I N W E E O H
    R A B M O T H D E C T N O T A C N I V F
  F G M O L T P T U E P O I Q U N R I S N T O O
  S B U T O M R O L R O T I S O P I V O R G R A
    G A O Y R D F T U I K R A B I O M A G M S
      N E S R U   Y G M G L   S F U L R E
                  I U Y B T
                  S C E
                  F
```

DIRECTIONS:

Use the clues below to find the insect words hidden in the cicada. The words may read frontward, backward, up, down, and diagonally.

1. The larva of this insect often spins a cocoon: _ _ _ _ _
2. An insect goes through many changes to become an _ _ _ _ _ _ _.
3. Nymphs and larvae can't fly because they don't have fully developed _ _ _ _ _ _ _.
4. The larva of this insect makes a chrysalis: _ _ _ _ _ _ _ _ _ _.
5. The changes an insect goes through as it grows are called

   _ _ _ _ _ _ _ _ _ _ _ _ _ _ _.
6. The nymphs of many aquatic insects breathe with _ _ _ _ _ _.
7. The first stage in an insect's life cycle is the _ _ _ _.
8. An insect that changes in 4 life stages—egg, larva, pupa, adult—goes through
   _ _ _ _ _ _ _ _ _ metamorphosis.
9. In complete metamorphosis, the egg hatches into the _ _ _ _ _ _.
10. An insect that changes in 3 life stages—egg, nymph, adult—goes through _ _ _ _ _ _ _ _,
    or incomplete, metamorphosis.
11. To grow, an insect must _ _ _ _ _, or shed its exoskeleton.
12. A _ _ _ _ _ _ is the young form of an insect that goes through incomplete or simple
    metamorphosis.
13. Female insects deposit their eggs through an _ _ _ _ _ _ _ _ _ _ _ _ _.
14. A moth or butterfly larva is called a _ _ _ _ _ _ _ _ _ _ _.
15. The _ _ _ _ _ is the resting stage of complete metamorphosis.
16. The larva of a beetle is sometimes called a _ _ _ _ _ _.
17. The larva of a fly is sometimes called a _ _ _ _ _ _ _.

FINDING A PLACE TO LIVE

 lmost a million different kinds of insects have already been discovered. And entomologists estimate that there are many times as many waiting to be found. There are more kinds of insects than all other animals put together.

Insects have managed to invade almost every habitat in the world. In fact it's almost impossible to find a place where there are no insects. You can find insects living on seashores, in forests, in deserts, on mountains, and even a few on the surface of the ocean. You can find them swimming in water, hiding in snowy banks and under leaves, living in caves, boring into wood or fruit, living inside plant stems, hitching rides on other animals, munching on plants, and flying in the air. They seem to be everywhere.

The activities in this section will focus on what an insect needs to survive and how an insect's habitat provides for these needs. Here are some concepts that will be reinforced in the activities:

Habitat: An animal's home is called its *habitat.* And just like all animals, insects live in habitats that provide them with food, shelter, water, and space to mate, lay eggs, and grow. Each insect has specific environmental needs that ease the competition with other insects. For example, the needs of a tent caterpillar are much different from the needs of a flea. Fleas survive by sucking blood from a warm host. Tent caterpillars survive by eating tree leaves and building a silken tent in the tree for protection. Some insects, such as cockroaches, are very adaptable and can live in many different kinds of habitats. Others, such as lice, need a very specific type of habitat in order to survive.

Food: The best way to tell what an insect eats is by taking a close look at its mouth. An insect's mouth is made up of several parts all working together. Each part is adapted to fit the eating needs of the insect.

Most insects either have chewing or sucking mouthparts or a combination or variation of both kinds. Chewing insects have jaws, called *mandibles,* that move sideways, not up and down as ours do. The jaws of some chewing beetles are so strong that they can bite through lead and copper.

Many insects have piercing-sucking mouthparts. These are adapted for sucking animal blood or plant sap, depending on the type of insect.

Some insects, such as flies, have lapping-sucking mouthparts. The end of a fly's mouth looks like a sponge and soaks up liquid food.

Moths and butterflies have a long tubelike mouth (*proboscis*) for sucking nectar from flowers. (See Copycat Page on page 34.)

MOUTHPARTS

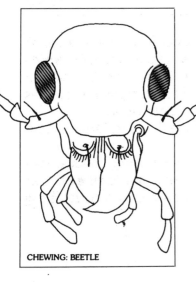

SUCKING: MOTH

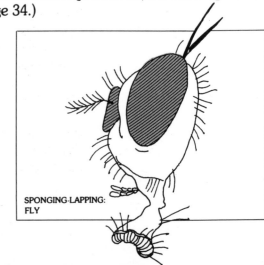

CHEWING: BEETLE

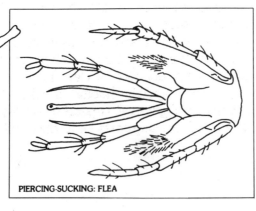

PIERCING-SUCKING: FLEA

SPONGING-LAPPING: FLY

The Need for Oxygen: Most insects get the oxygen they need from the air. But they do not have lungs as we do. Instead, air enters their bodies through tiny openings called *spiracles* on the sides of the abdomen and thorax. (There is often a pair of spiracles on each segment of the thorax and the abdomen.) The spiracles are connected to a network of tiny tubes, called *tracheae*, that spread to all parts of an insect's body. Air flows into the spiracles, then into the tubes. From there oxygen is absorbed by the cells in the insect's body. When the insect exhales, carbon dioxide passes out through the tubes and then out the spiracles. The openings to the spiracles can be closed by tiny flaps attached to muscles. For larger animals, this is not a very efficient way to breathe. But being so tiny, insects don't need as much oxygen as larger animals do.

Many of the insects that live in water have a very thin exoskeleton that allows dissolved oxygen in the water to seep into their bodies. The oxygen then enters the tracheal system. Other aquatic insects have gills that also absorb oxygen into their bodies or have breathing tubes that stick out of the water to get oxygen from the air. And some carry a bubble of air under the water as they dive.

Shelter: Insects live in places that provide them with shelter from enemies, harsh weather, and drying out. For some insects that means living underground, inside logs, in plant stems, or on other animals. Others make their homes in galls, fruits, or vegetables. And many insects build their own shelters. For example, honey bees build hives of wax and paper wasps make nests of chewed-up wood.

Water: Most insects get the water they need from the food they eat. Others drink water from ponds, streams, puddles, or dew drops.

Living Conditions: Each specific habitat provides certain living conditions—temperature, humidity, sunlight, soil, vegetation—that are suitable for the animals that live there. Each habitat supports only those animals adapted to its living conditions.

Note: Please skim through the Appendix for more information about how to explore different insect habitats.

Amazing Insect Mouths

Demonstrate how different insect mouths work using common tools and items found around the house.

Objectives:
Describe different insect mouthparts. Show how some insects use their mouthparts in feeding by comparing the mouthparts to familiar tools.

Ages:
Primary

Materials:
- *large pictures of house fly, grasshopper, female mosquito, and butterfly or moth*
- *pliers*
- *sponge*
- *toy syringe*
- *clear drinking glass or beaker*
- *food coloring (any color)*
- *enough soda straws for the group*
- *enough milk or juice for the group*
- *copies of page 34 (optional)*

Subject:
Science

If you were to compare a beetle's mouth to a butterfly's mouth, you'd see a big difference. Beetles have *chewing* mouthparts and butterflies have *sucking* mouthparts. Insects have different types of mouthparts because they feed on different types of food. In this activity, your group will be able to see that insects have different kinds of mouthparts and each type of mouth works in a different way.

Begin by asking your group some questions about how insects eat. For example, ask if insects have teeth. (Lots of children may say yes, since they may have been "bitten" by an insect.) Explain that insects don't have teeth as people and many other animals do. But many do have sharp jaws for tearing and chewing food.

Then ask if all insects eat the same things. (Different insects eat many different kinds of food such as blood, leaves, nectar, dead animals, manure, fungi, and wood, just to name a few. And to eat these foods, insects have developed different kinds of mouthparts.)

Next, hold up pictures of a grasshopper, house fly, mosquito, and butterfly and explain that each of these common insects has a different type of mouthpart. Then compare each of these insect mouths with the following tools and household items to demonstrate how each mouthpart works:

- A grasshopper's mouthparts work something like *pliers* to tear and chew plants. Their jaws move sideways, not up and down as people's do. (Hold the pliers sideways and work them back and forth.)
- Female mosquitoes use their needle-like mouthparts to draw up blood in much the same way as a doctor uses a *needle and syringe*. (Put a syringe into a glass or beaker containing colored water and draw some of it up. Use food coloring to color the water.)
- A house fly's mouthparts work like a *sponge* to soak up liquids. (Pour out a little water and sop it up with a sponge.)

As a nice ending to your discussion, let the group discover for themselves how butterflies and moths feed. Pass out straws and milk or fruit juice to each person. As you hold up a picture of a butterfly or moth, talk about how these insects often feed on nectar from flowers. Explain that the long, tongue-like mouthparts of many butterflies and moths are used as a straw would be to sip up the nectar. Now have your kids pretend to be butterflies and moths as they sip up their juice or milk "nectar."

For older children, pass out the "Amazing Mouths" Copycat Page on page 34.

Insect Bingo

Make special insect bingo cards and take a walk to play insect bingo.

Objectives:
Describe five places where insects live. Give examples of the ways insects find food, water, shelter, and a place to lay their eggs.

Ages:
Primary and Intermediate

Materials:
- *copies of Insect Bingo chart (page 32)*

(continued next page)

Insect Bingo is an exciting way to investigate insect habitats. Make enough copies of the bingo chart on page 32 for each person in the group to have one. Also pass out scissors, glue, and cardboard. Now have each student make up a game card, or "bug board," by cutting apart the chart squares and pasting them in a new arrangement on their sheet of paper or cardboard. (Each card will have the same items, but the items will be arranged in a different order.)

Now take a walk on a nature trail or in the schoolyard. Have the kids look for the items and insects that are shown on their sheets. When someone spots something on the sheet, discuss it in relation to an insect's habitat. For example, if a dragonfly is spotted, ask the children what it might eat or where it takes shelter in case of a storm. Or why it needs to live close to water. (Dragonflies lay their eggs in or near the water, and the nymphs that hatch live underwater in rivers, ponds, and lakes.) If someone sees an insect home, discuss how that home provides food, water, shelter, and a place to lay eggs for a particular type of insect. Also talk about the different types of insects that might live there.

Have everyone put an X over the things

on his or her board as they are spotted. The first person to get a whole line crossed (up, down, diagonally) wins the game.

To make the cards permanent and reusable have the kids paste the squares onto heavy cardboard. Laminate the cards or cover them with clear contact paper. Then have them use special grease pencils to X the squares so that the X s can be easily wiped off and the cards used again.

Who Lives Here?

Complete an insect habitat activity sheet.

Objective:
Give examples of several different insect microhabitats.

Ages:
Intermediate

Materials:
- copies of the "Who Lives Here?" worksheet on page 33
- insect field guides and textbooks
- pencils and colored markers

Subject:
Science

There are many different kinds of major habitats in the world, such as forests, mountains, streams, deserts, swamps, rivers, tundra, and seashores. But in each of these large habitat areas there are many smaller *microhabitats* that support many different types of creatures, especially small animals. For example, in a forest habitat, some insects spend their entire lives in the leaf litter on the forest floor or inside a rotting log. Each is considered a microhabitat of the forest because each provides food, shelter, water, and enough space for the insects' needs.

To get your kids thinking about microhabitats and where insects live, pass out copies of the "Who Lives Here?" worksheet. (You can have the kids work in teams or individually.) The object is to find a type of insect that lives in each microhabitat listed on the left side of the worksheet. Then they have to fill in the name of the insect and what it eats and draw a sketch of the insect.

Many different insects live in each microhabitat, so everyone's chart will have different answers. If you want to be more specific, you can fill in the column "What It Eats" before you hand it out.

Give each person (or team) time in the library to learn to use simple field guides and insect reference books to find out where insects live and what they look like.

When everyone has finished, go through the list and discuss each habitat area and how it fills the needs of each insect. Compare the insects listed for each habitat. How are they the same? How are they different? Ask the kids why insects that live in the same microhabitat eat different things. (In that way they don't compete for limited amounts of food.) You can also discuss how each insect is especially adapted to living in a certain microhabitat. (mole crickets: digging legs, chewing mouthparts; praying mantids: grasping front legs, chewing mouthparts; fleas: sucking mouthparts, flattened bodies for squeezing between animals' hairs)

Invent an Insect

Write about and draw fantasy insects and describe their habitats.

Objective:
Describe several ways insects are adapted to their environment.

Ages:
All

Materials:
- index cards and paper
- pencils, crayons, paints

Subjects:
Science and Art

Once your kids have learned all about real insects, they might want to invent their own insects. Write these or similar directions on index cards. For example, your "invention cards" might describe habitats such as these:
- invent an insect that lives in water
- invent an insect that lives in a cave
- invent an insect that lives in soil
- invent an insect that lives in dry sand
- invent an insect that lives in snow
- invent an insect that lives in wood
(continued next page)

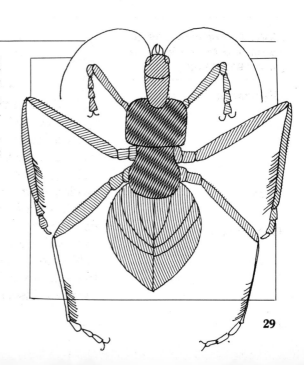

Then have the inventors describe the following:

1. what it eats
2. what might try to eat it
3. how it moves and defends itself
4. special adaptations it has for living in its habitat

Then have each of them draw a picture of his or her insect in each stage of its life cycle, illustrating the insect's metamorphosis and what it looks like as an adult.

You can also make up different kinds of invention cards that are more specific. Here are some examples:

- invent an insect that lives inside an acorn
- invent an insect that can outrun you
- invent an insect that you can see through
- invent an insect that doesn't look like an insect
- invent an insect that you wouldn't want to touch
- invent an insect that could live on the moon
- invent an insect that lives on another insect

After the activity, have each person present his or her "creation" to the rest of the group. How many of them drew insects that look similar to insects that really exist? Have each person name his or her insect. (As a variation, you can have the kids make a model of their insects using modeling clay or dough. See page 57 for directions.)

Dipping for Aquatic Insects

Make aquatic dip nets and go dipping for insects.

Objectives:
Identify several aquatic insects. Describe how aquatic insects are adapted to living in the water.

Ages:
Intermediate

Materials:
- *same as for butterfly net (see page 58 in the Appendix) but use muslin for the entire net and make the net a little shorter.*
- *white baking dishes, bowls, or collecting pans*
- *strainer (optional)*
- *broomstick or other long pole (optional)*
- *duct or plastic insulation tape (optional)*

Subject:
Science

Safety Note:
Be careful not to let children get too close to deep water or climb on slippery rocks. Shallow ponds and streams are safer.

In order to watch and study aquatic insects up close, you need to catch some—and dip nets work great! Dip the net into the pond or stream, being sure to scoop up some bottom mud and water plants. In a stream, place your net just downstream of a rock as you lift the corner of the rock. Some of the critters hiding under the rock may be washed into the net. Children can do this alone or they can work in pairs. (Put the rocks back in place when you are through.)

Sift through the net by hand, searching for insect larvae, nymphs, and adults. Also look for insect eggs attached to plants and floating twigs.

For a better look, dump the contents of the dip net into a white pan. The insects will crawl around and be easier to spot against the white background.

You can also make a strainer dip stick by fastening the handle of a large kitchen sieve to a broom stick or long pole. Fasten it securely with duct tape or plastic insulation tape. (This kind of net is best for straining the water. It's not strong enough for scooping up things from the bottom.)

Note: Make sure to return all insects to the water when the activity is over.

For more information on how to identify aquatic insects see *Pond Life, A Golden Nature Guide* by George Reid, Golden

Press, New York, 1967. For more activities about aquatic insects, see OBIS Modules on *Water Striders, Damsels and Dragons,* and *Too Many Mosquitoes.* (Check the Appendix for OBIS address.)

WATERY DISCUSSIONS

After watching aquatic insects and learning how to use dip nets, see if your group can make some observations and comparisons about what they found and saw. Here are some discussion questions:

- How are aquatic insects adapted to swimming? (Some, such as water boatmen, have oarlike legs covered with hairs, and others, such as stonefly nymphs, have streamlined bodies.)

- How do aquatic nymphs, larvae, and adults breathe? (Some have gills along the abdomen or thorax, some carry a bubble of air taken from the surface, some use breathing tubes, and some must come to the surface to breathe.)
- What do aquatic insects eat? (Dragonfly nymphs eat other insects, small fish, and tadpoles; mosquito larvae are scavengers; waterbugs catch other insects.)
- What animals eat aquatic insects? (fish, turtles, other insects, water snakes, fishing spiders, water birds)
- What happens to insects in a fast-moving stream? Do they get washed away? (Many attach themselves to rocks and logs. Some have flattened bodies to lessen water resistance.)

Getting into Galls

Make a gall catcher to observe which insects are gall makers.

Objectives:
Describe different types of plant galls and explain how plant galls form. Recognize that galls provide a home for developing insects.

Ages:
All

Materials:
- *mesh screen*
- *sturdy thread and needle*
- *sharp knife*

Subject:
Science

Galls are those strange-looking swellings you often see on plants. They come in all shapes, sizes, and colors, from pink, round, and woolly to flat and spiny. Galls can be caused by many different things, such as fungi, nematode worms, or mites. But many of the common types of galls are caused by insects.

You can find galls on different kinds of plants and on different parts of plants. Some are found on flowers, leaves, stems, bark, and roots.

An insect gall forms when a female insect lays her eggs in a plant. When an egg hatches, the larva that comes out secretes a special chemical that causes the plant part to grow in a weird, unnatural way. Certain moths, wasps, and flies are the most common gall makers and each species makes a differently shaped gall. The gall provides food, shelter, and water for the growing larva. Many larvae will eat and grow inside the same gall during the summer, pupate in the winter, and emerge as adults the following spring.

To take a closer look at galls, search with your group for galls on trees, shrubs, and flowers. (Oak, willow, hickory, cottonwood, poplar, and cherry are good trees to search; blackberry, rose, and

goldenrod are also gall-forming plants.)

When you find a gall, have the kids look to see if there is a tiny hole on the outside of it. If there is, the adult has probably already emerged. If not, you can watch the gall and find out what insect made it.

The best way to see galls "hatch" is to leave them outside on the plant and make a gall catcher out of mesh wire screen. Sew the screen cage around the gall to form a basket. Check your trap every day, if possible. When the adult crawls out of the gall it will be trapped inside the screen. Watch the insect up close through the screen and see if you can tell what kind it is. (Many gall insects are very tiny.) You can also try to bring the gall inside. Put the cut end of a leaf or twig in water so the plant stays alive, and set it inside a glass tank that has a screened-in top. Watch it every day to see what comes out. You can also cut open large galls, such as oak-apple and goldenrod, to show your kids the developing larvae.

It may be that the emerging insect is not the one that made the gall. Many species of insects do not make galls themselves, but lay eggs in galls made by other types of insects. And many insects are parasites on gall insects, laying eggs on the gall insect larvae.

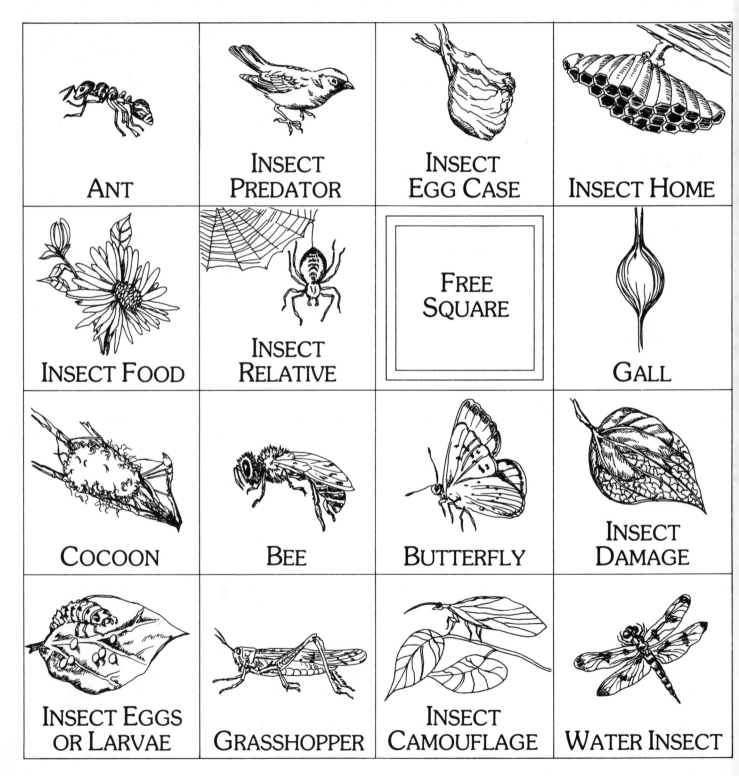

ANT	INSECT PREDATOR	INSECT EGG CASE	INSECT HOME
INSECT FOOD	INSECT RELATIVE	FREE SQUARE	GALL
COCOON	BEE	BUTTERFLY	INSECT DAMAGE
INSECT EGGS OR LARVAE	GRASSHOPPER	INSECT CAMOUFLAGE	WATER INSECT

WHERE IT LIVES	ITS NAME	WHAT IT EATS	WHAT IT LOOKS LIKE
In a tree	Acorn weevil	Acorns	
In tall grass			
In a garden			
On a cactus			
In your house			

Insect mouths are amazing:
Some suck and some chew,
Some pierce and some sponge,
And some even slurp goo.

Each mouth is a tool
Used to help insects eat
Whatever they need,
Whether blood, plants, or meat.

We've picked out three insects,
Described all their foods,
Then drawn them as tools
Or as things people use.

Can you guess what they are
From the verses below?
(All three crazy insects
Are ones that you know.)

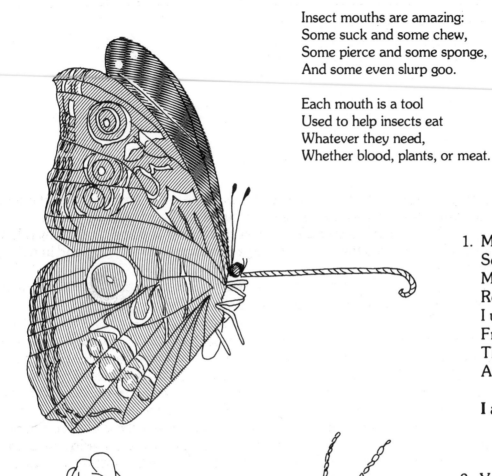

1. My body is covered with
   Scales, not with skin;
   My mouth's like a straw,
   Round, long, and thin;
   I unroll this neat "tongue"
   From under my chin.
   Then I suck up some nectar
   And roll it back in.

   I am a _____

2. You'll find me in fields
   'Cause it's leaves that I munch.
   And if you should grab me
   I'll spit up my lunch.
   My jaws are like pliers
   To chew, tear, and crunch,
   And sometimes I'm a problem
   'Cause I eat such a bunch.

   I am a _____

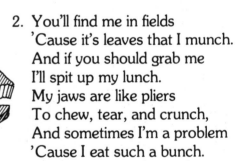

3. My mate sucks up nectar,
   But I go for blood.
   I'll get you in swamps
   When you're tromping through mud.
   My mouth's like a needle,
   As sharp as a pin,
   And I'll suck up your blood
   Through a hole in your skin.

   I am a _____

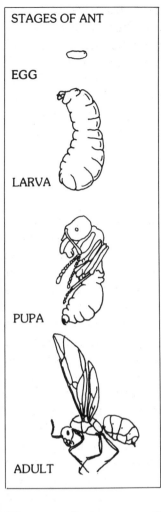

STAGES OF ANT

EGG

LARVA

PUPA

ADULT

of their lives.

4. Most ants have antennae that are segmented and bent in the middle (elbowed antennae). They use their antennae as smell, touch, and taste organs.

5. Many kinds of animals eat ants, including anteaters, woodpeckers, aardvarks, skunks, and snakes.

After the sugar . . .

1. and 2.—see worksheet

3. Ants communicate with each other by releasing odors into the air or by laying down a scent trail. They also vibrate their bodies when they are excited. Both the odors and the vibrations can be picked up by other ants' antennae.

Ants also regurgitate drops of food, which are then transferred among the workers. This food contains chemical substances (similar to our hormones) that communicate what the ant senses.

4. Worker ants have a special stomach (the crop) for storing nectar, honeydew from aphids, and other food. They also have very strong muscles that help them carry and push large bits of food. Most ants have strong jaws with notches for cutting and a tongue-like structure for sucking.

5. Ants usually follow a scent trail (laid down by other ants) to and from the colony.

BRANCHING OUT: POETRY

After watching and studying ants, have each person write a poem about ants. The poem can describe how ants look, how an ant colony functions, how ants communicate, or a combination of thoughts and ideas.

You might also want to have your group write a story based on life in the colony. Here are some suggestions:

- compare an ant colony to your neighborhood
- write about a day in the life of an ant worker or a queen
- make up an ant fantasy, such as "A Trip to the Planet of the Ants"

You can also copy the ant maze on page 42 and hand it out to reinforce your ant detective activities.

Population Count

Using hula hoops as markers, estimate the size of an insect population and graph the results.

Objectives:
Describe how an insect population is sampled and how the sample is used to estimate a population size. Explain the importance of large numbers of individuals in assuring insect survival.

Ages:
Intermediate and Advanced

Materials:
- *pencils and paper*
- *hula hoops or string*
- *jars or plastic bags*

(continued next page)

I f you take a walk through a field on a warm summer day, you will see insects everywhere—crickets, grasshoppers, butterflies, aphids, beetles, and many more. In some one-acre plots there can be over a million or more insects, chirping and buzzing away. It's hard to imagine that so many creatures—even such tiny ones—are living in one place!

In these activities, your group will explore insect populations—how they are counted, why they are important, and how they change season by season.

HULA HOOP COUNT #1

Ask your group how many insects they think live in their backyard or schoolyard. Write down their guesses and then ask them how they would find out how close their guesses are to the actual number of insects. Someone will probably say, "Just count them!" But explain that there are so many insects that it would be impossible to count them all. For example, there could be over 1000 aphids on just one plant.

Instead of counting all the insects in the field, scientists estimate how many insects there are by counting the insects in small samples and then estimating how many there would be in the whole field.

Tell your group they will become *entomologists* for the day to find out how many insects are in a given area. Follow these steps to conduct your count:

1. Find a nearby open area, such as the schoolyard, a backyard, a vacant lot, or a field. Divide the group into four teams and give each team plastic bags or jars for collecting, pencils and paper, and a hula hoop. (If you don't have hula hoops, you can have each group

- *tweezers or forceps (optional)*
- *index cards*

Subjects:
Science and Math

measure off a square using string and sticks.)

Pick a common insect that lives in the area. (In this example, we will use a grasshopper.) Tell each team they are going to try to find out how many grasshoppers live in the field. To do that, each team is going to sample one small area.

2. Have each team toss out a hula hoop. Each hula hoop will be the boundary for that team's study plot. Explain that each team must count all the grasshoppers that are in the boundary set by the hoop. They can collect the insects temporarily in their jars or bags to avoid counting the same grasshopper twice. Have them check under leaves, on the top of the soil, in the grass, on flowerheads, and in the air.

When each team has finished, have them release their grasshoppers and gather back together in a group. As each team reports on how many insects they counted, discuss the following questions:
- Why did some plots have more grass-

hoppers than others? (Some plots may have had more food for the grasshoppers or better places to hide. Some groups may have counted more carefully. Some parts of the field might have fewer predators.)
- What were some of the problems in trying to count all the grasshoppers? (They kept hopping away, probably counted some twice, could not see them all, some were very tiny, etc.)
- Can you think of a way that you could figure out how many grasshoppers were in the whole field? What else would you have to know? (They could explain that they would need to somehow figure up how many hula hoops could fit in the field and then multiply the average number of grasshoppers per hula hoop by the total number of hula hoops that could fit. For example, if there were an average of 15 grasshoppers in a hula hoop and the field could hold 80 hula hoops, multiplying 80 by 15 would give the approximate number of grasshoppers in the field. Remember, this would be just a rough estimate.)

HULA HOOP COUNT #2

Now try another method. Have each team throw out their hula hoops again. But this time assign each group a different insect. For example, Team 1 could be crickets, Team 2 could be ants, and so on. Have them again count the number of insects in their hoop and write down what they get. Then compare the counts and discuss the following questions:

- Why are there more of one type of insect than another? (The study area might be better suited for certain kinds of insects. For example, there might be more food for crickets, better hiding places for ants, better places to find nectar for

butterflies, etc. Some insects need more open space. Some insects have larger populations than others.)
- Were some insects harder to count than others? Why? (Some are better camouflaged than others, some are smaller, some are harder to catch, etc.)
- Why do you think some insects have such large populations? (Insects, like many other invertebrates, have large populations as survival insurance. Even if a disaster such as a storm or disease epidemic strikes, there will likely be at least a few individuals that survive to mate, lay eggs, and regenerate the populations.)

GRAPHING A DIFFERENCE

To practice making a line graph and a bar graph, have your group try these graphing activities:

- Have a grasshopper count (like the one

in Part #1) once a month for the whole year. Keep a record of the number of grasshoppers and then make a line graph showing how the numbers change month by month.

YEARLY GRASSHOPPER COUNT

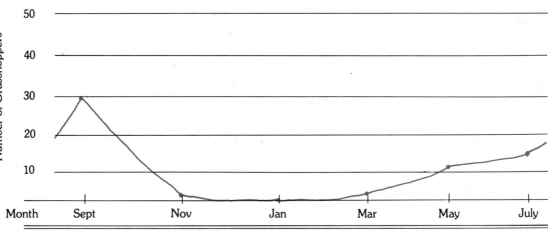

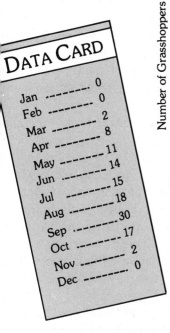

DATA CARD

Jan	0
Feb	0
Mar	2
Apr	8
May	11
Jun	14
Jul	15
Aug	18
Sep	30
Oct	17
Nov	2
Dec	0

(Since it's sometimes difficult to sample all year, you might want to pass out data cards with fake data on them for the children to graph. See the example.)

• Give each person an information card that has a list of different kinds of insects and how many occur in a sample plot.

Then have each person use the information on the card to make a simple bar graph. See if each person can guess what habitat the data might have come from.

DATA CARD

Bees	8
Wasps	6
Ants	14
Grasshoppers	13
Flies	3
Beetles	11

INSECTS IN A SAMPLE PLOT

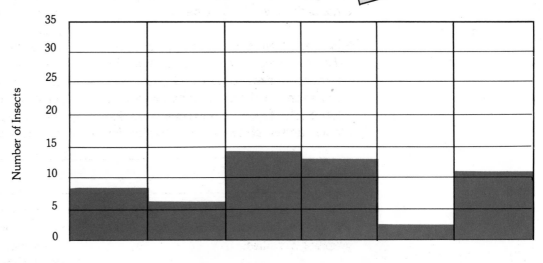

AN ANT'S A-MAZING WORLD

Help the ant find a safe path to the food in the meadow. Then help it take the food to the food room in its colony.

DEAD GRASSHOPPERS — GOOD FOOD FOR ANTS!

DON'T GET SQUISHED!

HUNGRY WOLF SPIDER

TOO CLOSE TO ANOTHER ANT COLONY!

HUNGRY FLICKER

SHREW ON THE PROWL!

EGG HATCHING ROOM

PUPA ROOM

FOOD ROOM

TRASH ROOM

QUEEN

THE HUNGRY BIRD

Insects are food for birds, snakes, frogs, toads, other insects, shrews, bears, fish, and many other animals. Draw TWO insects this hungry bird might find to eat in this field. Can you make one *camouflaged?*

Name_____ Date_____

1. What color are most of the ants? _____

2. Does an ant have hair? _____

3. Are the ants all the same size and shape? If not, how are they different?
_____
_____

4. Draw a picture of an ant antenna in the box.

5. Draw something that might eat an ant.

After the sugar . . .
1. Did the ants find the sugar?_____
2. How long did it take them to discover it? _____
3. How do ants communicate with each other? _____
_____
4. Are the ants carrying food back to the hill? If so, how are they carrying it? _____
_____
5. Do the ants seem to follow a path or randomly walk back and forth into the ant nest?
_____
_____

PEOPLE AND INSECTS

any children (and adults) will often ask "What good is an insect?" That's because most people connect insects with bad things, such as diseases, stings, and crop destruction. It's no wonder that the saying "The only good insect is a dead one " has become so popular.

What most people don't stop to think about are the positive ways that insects have influenced our society and the reasons they are so important to people and other living things.

Below we've listed some of the "good" and "bad" points about insects. The list indicates the importance of insects in our lives and how they fit in with other living things. (It's important to realize that these are people's value systems. There is no "good" or "bad" in nature.)

WHY PEOPLE LIKE INSECTS

- are very important plant pollinators, especially of fruit and other crop plants
- provide honey, shellac, wax, and silk
- help control other pests
- provide food for many birds, fish, and other animals—including people
- used to treat diseases in people
- provide information on heredity, evolution, biochemistry, and other important science topics
- are good indicators of water pollution
- are fascinating to watch; inspiring to poets, writers, photographers, designers, and students

WHY PEOPLE DON'T LIKE INSECTS

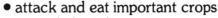

- attack and eat important crops
- spread plant diseases
- transmit diseases to people and other animals
- infest households as pests
- bite, sting, stink, etc.
- ruin stored crops, such as flour, popcorn, rice, etc.
- require use of pesticides and other poisons, which often harm other animals

The activities in this chapter focus on the many ways insects influence our lives—both positively and negatively. Here is some background information about controlling harmful insects by using *Integrated Pest Management* (IPM).

WHAT'S IPM?

It used to be that when people had a problem with insects they pulled out the poisons. Chemical pesticides seemed like the fastest and easiest solution to a pest problem. But as many people have now learned, these chemicals can have terrible side effects on all living things. Some kill many kinds of animals besides the pests. Many seep into the soil, contaminating ground water supplies, lakes, rivers, and food sources. And many persist for a long time, poisoning the environment for hundreds of years.

Today, entomologists are encouraging people to use another way to control pests called IPM. IPM uses a variety of pest control techniques to create a more efficient and safe way to manage insect pests. Here are some of the IPM techniques entomologists are working with:

- **Natural predators:** introducing the types of animals that will naturally gobble up pests. Ladybugs, praying mantids, garter snakes, toads, and purple martins are all examples of natural predators that eat insect pests.
- **Natural parasites:** introducing bacteria, viruses, and insect parasites that will kill pests but won't harm other types of animals.
- **Mixed plantings:** planting mixed stands of trees or crops instead of planting large areas with just one type of plant. Mixed stands are not as susceptible to insect damage.
- **Sterile insects:** releasing thousands of sterile males or females of a pest species. When fertile insects mate with sterile partners, they don't produce offspring.
- **Habitat changes:** changing the habitat to physically control many pest species. For example, by getting rid of all the old tires in your neighborhood you can cut down on the number of mosquitoes breeding in your area. (The tires fill up with rainwater, making perfect breeding sites for mosquitoes.)
- **Insect hormones:** using insect hormones to prevent an insect from growing into a sexually mature adult. (Just as in people, hormones control growth and development in insects.)
- **Chemicals:** using pesticides only as needed. In IPM, chemicals are just one small part of the whole plan. By studying an insect's life cycle, just the right amount of pesticide at just the right time can be used effectively. Less pesticide and careful application mean a more healthful environment and better pest control.
- **Timing:** regulating planting and harvesting to avoid those times when insects are most abundant and damaging.
- **Mechanical:** removing eggs, larvae, cocoons, and adults from plants by hand.
- **Pheromones:** using natural and synthetic pheromones to attract or confuse insect pests.

I Like Insects Because . . .

Discuss how people feel about insects.

Objective:
Describe how insects help people and how insects harm people.

Ages:
Primary

Materials:
- *pictures of insects*

Subjects:
Science and Social Studies

Sit in a circle with your children and have them close their eyes. Tell them to think about butterflies, bees, walking sticks, ants, beetles, and other kinds of insects. While their eyes are closed, spread out pictures of insects in the center. Then have them open their eyes and look through the pictures for a few minutes. This will get them to start thinking about the many different kinds of insects.

Now explain some of the reasons people don't like insects. (They sting, bite, eat people's food, eat people's clothes, look creepy, etc.) Point to the pictures of the insects that may cause these problems. Now, starting with the person on your right, tell the kids to finish the sentence, "I don't like insects because . . . "

Encourage the kids to share a negative insect experience they've had after saying why they don't like insects. Go around the circle so that each person gets a chance to complete the sentence and share an insect experience.

Do the same thing for the reasons people like insects. Your examples could include: they're pretty, they come in all kinds of colors, they make honey, they are fun to watch, they help plants. Again point to the pictures of the insects that are beneficial in some way. This time go around the circle and have each person finish the sentence, "I like insects because . . . "

Afterward, discuss the group's comments. Explain that insects do create problems for people and some are pests, but point out that they are also very important as food for animals, as pollinators, as honey makers, and in many other ways. (See pages 46 and 52 for more information about people and insects.)

A Taste of Honey

Sample different kinds of honey and make an easy honey and peanut butter snack.

Objective:
Explain how honey is produced and why there are variations in honey flavor and color.

Ages:
All

Materials:
- *several different types of honey (you can get these at a health food store or from a local beekeeper)*
- *crackers or spoons*
- *honey bears (plastic squeeze bottles)*
- *ingredients for honey balls (see "Natural Nibbles" on page 48)*

Subjects:
Science and Nutrition

One of the most delicious products we get from insects is honey, a natural sweetener. The reason honey is so special is that only honey bees can make it, using flower nectar and adding a special chemical from their bodies. Here's how they do it:

1. First the worker bees collect nectar from flowers, sucking it up with their tongues and storing it in their honey stomachs, called *crops.*
2. Once their stomachs are full, the worker bees go back to the hive and transfer the nectar to other worker bees. (They do this by regurgitating the nectar into the mouths of the hive bees.) The hive bees then store the nectar in cells in the comb.
3. To make honey, the hive bees work with one drop of nectar at a time. Each bee takes a drop into its mouth, adds a special chemical called an *enzyme,* and blows air into the drop—almost like blowing bubbles. The blowing gets rid of some of the water (by evaporation),

and, in conjunction with the enzyme, turns the drop into honey.

Each type of nectar makes a different flavor and color of honey. For example, if the bees collect nectar only from clover, they'll make clover honey, which is a light, mild honey. (Since farmers use honey bees to pollinate clover fields, especially in the Midwest, clover honey is one of the most common types of honey available.)

If the bee hive is in a buckwheat patch, the bees will make buckwheat honey. Buckwheat honey has a very strong, bold taste and is much darker than clover honey.

In the wild, many bees collect nectar from different kinds of wildflowers, including tree blossoms. These bees make a honey called wildflower honey.

TASTE TEST

Describe this honey-making process to your group and then have a taste test. Try to have a light-colored, a dark-colored, and an exotic honey, such as lime or palmetto honey. Pour the honey into honey bears (plastic squeeze jars) so it will be easier to give all the kids a taste.

Pass out crackers (or spoons) and put some honey on each. Have the kids taste one kind of honey at a time.

After they taste the honey, have them describe the differences. Which honey did they like best? What are some adjectives that describe honey? See if they can guess why one type of honey is a light color while another is darker. (The color and flavor depend on the type of nectar.) What other animals like to eat honey? (ants, flies, mice, bears, and badgers) Ask the kids what they like to eat with honey.

CLOVER HONEY

BUCKWHEAT HONEY

ORANGE BLOSSOM HONEY

NATURAL NIBBLES: HONEY BALLS

Use the leftover honey to make honey balls with your group. It's a nutritious snack that uses honey as the sweetener. You will need:

- 1/3 cup honey
- 1/2 cup peanut butter
- 1/2 cup powdered milk
- 1 envelope of unflavored gelatin (optional)

Sunflower seeds, raisins, or anything else you want to add
Granola or wheat germ

Mix the first five ingredients together. Have the kids each roll a ball of the mixture in either granola or wheat germ, which has been spread out on paper plates and placed around the room.

Take a Trip

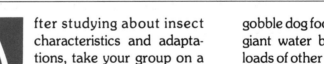

Visit an insect zoo or an insect exhibit at a museum.

Objective:
Describe an insect zoo.

Ages:
All

Subject:
Science

After studying about insect characteristics and adaptations, take your group on a trip to one of the many places listed below.

- Visit an insect zoo. Here they will have a chance to see many different kinds of insects close up. Insect zoos are springing up in museums, zoos, and nature centers all across the country. Visitors get a firsthand look at many common species of insects and other arthropods (and often a firsthand feel).

At many insect zoos, feeding times are posted. Kids can watch cockroaches gobble dog food, butterflies suck nectar, giant water bugs snatch crickets, and loads of other hungry arthropods eating. Many also have creatures from other parts of the country or the world, such as cockroaches from Madagascar and tarantulas from South America.

Here are some insect zoos and museums with insect exhibits that you can visit if you get a chance:

- The Insect Zoo at the Smithsonian's Museum of Natural History in Washington, D.C.
- The World of Insects at the zoo in Cincinnati, Ohio

- The Insect Zoo at the zoo in San Francisco, California
- The Washington Park Insect Zoo in Portland, Oregon
- The Arizona-Sonora Desert Museum in Tucson, Arizona
- The Memphis Pink Palace Museum in Memphis, Tennessee
- Discovery Center Museum in Fort Lauderdale, Florida
- North Carolina Museum of Natural History in Raleigh, North Carolina
- Indianapolis Children's Museum in Indiana
- Manitoba Museum of Man and Nature in Winnipeg, Manitoba
- Bishop Museum Hall of Discovery in Honolulu, Hawaii

- Take a trip to a nature center. Many have honey bee and ant observation colonies where your kids can get a close-up look at insects. Many nature centers also have naturalist-led programs about honey bees, social insects, or insects in general.
- Visit a beekeeper. In many areas there are local beekeepers who would be happy to present a "bee talk" to your group.
- For a different perspective, invite a pest control representative to come to your class or club meeting and present a program about insect pests. You also might want to visit the company's headquarters.
- Check with your local universities to see if any have an entomology department. Maybe a professor or graduate student would present an insect program and show your kids how to make an insect collection.
- Call your county extension agent for information or to ask someone to give an insect program.

Insects on Stage

Act out a play or conduct interviews to learn about insect pests.

Objective:
Show, through drama, several ways insects affect people's lives.

Ages:
Primary, Intermediate, and Advanced

Materials:
- *paper*
- *pencils*
- *reference books about insects*
- *materials to make props and costumes (cardboard, paint, markers, paper bags, etc.)*

Subjects:
Language Arts, Creative Drama, Science

An exciting way for kids to learn about insects and their relationship with people is by putting on skits, plays, and TV programs. Divide the group into three teams and have each team pick an insect or a group of insects they would like to learn more about. (You might want to supply them with a list of ideas to choose from. Insects that affect people directly are especially instructive, such as mosquitoes, honey bees, cockroaches, Mediterranean fruit flies, or house flies.)

Explain that each team will have to stage an interview, put on a play, or conduct a live TV show about its insect(s). Their presentation should include the following information: what the insects eat, where they live, what type of life cycle they have, whether they are pests, whether they are beneficial in some way, how they are managed, and how they affect people's lives.

After the teams have researched their topics, have them decide how they want to present the information to the rest of the group in an entertaining and educational way. Here are two ideas:

SAMPLE INTERVIEW WITH A GYPSY MOTH

Possible characters:
- **reporter—Arthur O. Pod**
- **gypsy moth caterpillar—Cruncher**
- **adult gypsy moth—Flutter**
- **white oak tree—Oakee**

Reporter: Welcome to WBUG News. My name is Arthur O. Pod and have I got a story for you viewers out there. We have an exclusive live oak interview with Cruncher the gypsy moth caterpillar.

We're happy to have you crawl by our program tonight, Cruncher.

Cruncher: I'm happy to be here. At least your listeners will get to hear our side of the story for a change.

Reporter: As you know, gypsy moths have been in the news a lot all over the East. Can you tell us, Cruncher, how you got to the United States in the first place? I remember a time when no one had ever heard of a gypsy moth.

Cruncher: Well, it's not my fault we're

49

Cruncher: Oh, the trees in this country are just as tasty as the ones back in Europe. We especially like oaks and hickories, but when things get tough, we're not too fussy at all.

The interview could continue with Arthur asking questions like these:

Reporter: How old are you, Cruncher?
Reporter: What happens when you change into a pupa?
Reporter: Can you describe your parents for the audience?
Reporter: How many eggs did your mother lay?
Reporter: How did you guys spread so quickly? Why, there seem to be gypsy moth caterpillars almost everywhere.
Reporter: Why aren't you a problem over in Europe, where your ancestors came from?

For more information on gypsy moth activities, see the *Gypsy Moth Workbook* reference in the Appendix on page 62.

here. In the 1850s a scientist brought some gypsy moths from Europe. (That's where we really belong.) Well, while the scientist was trying to do some experiments with them, some escaped. Crawled right past his nose . . .
Reporter: What kinds of things did you find to eat here?

A Short Play Idea

Possible characters:
- squash bug: **Bugsy**
- aphids: **The Sucking Sisters**
- ladybug beetle: **Tubs**
- praying mantid: **Jaws**
- bluebird: **Wormer**
- toads: **Warty and Hopper**
- vegetables (props, or kids dressed as vegetables)

Title: An Integrated Plot in the Garden

Synopsis: Insects get to talking about what integrated pest management is and which biological controls can be used, such as using more ladybugs and praying mantids, planting certain plants next to each other, and setting up bird houses nearby to attract bird predators.

Scene I: In the Joneses' Garden

Bugsy (sitting on a zucchini): Oh wow, this is the life!
Aphids: You said it! Lots of fresh juicy stems to suck.
Bugsy: Fat, ripe zucchini to chomp. It's a good thing the Jones family hasn't found out about it!

Aphids: Found out about what?
Bugsy: Integrated Pest Management.
Aphids: What?
Bugsy: Integrated Pest Management, or IPM as it's called.
Aphids: How do you know so much about this IPM?
Bugsy: Do you know Jose, that Mexican bean beetle that wandered through yesterday? He told me all about it.
Aphids: What did he tell you?
Bugsy: The Bishops—the next door neighbors—started doing all kinds of things to their garden to get rid of pests like us. Jose didn't want to stick around to see if it worked.
Aphids: I've heard the Bishops used to have the worst garden in the neighborhood.
Bugsy: Not anymore . . .
(One of the kids brings a sign by that says: SUDDENLY, TUBS THE LADYBUG CRAWLED UP TO THE ZUCCHINI PATCH.)
Aphids: Oh no, a ladybug. We're in trouble now. (The aphids tremble and look scared.)

Tubs: Don't worry, my tasty little morsels. I've had my fill today. I've eaten 42 aphids and I can't crawl another inch. I'm stuffed!

Bugsy: Where were you?

Tubs: Over in the Bishops' garden, in aphid heaven. Although it's not too bad over here either.

Bugsy: Well, maybe you can fill us in. What are they doing over there? We've heard all kinds of things.

Tubs: Remember when the Murphys used all that disgusting poison? Well, it killed some of the pests all right. But it also killed a lot of insects that are helpful to people, like praying mantids and honey bees. And it even made their kid sick.

Aphids: We remember. It killed a lot of our relatives too.

Tubs: Well, the Bishops talked to an insect expert to find out what they could do instead of using poisons.

Bugsy: And what did the expert say?

Tubs: She gave them all kinds of ideas about getting rid of disgusting "pests" like you.

Bugsy: Well, I'm going over there to see for myself.

Scene II: In the Bishops' Garden

As the curtain opens, a praying mantid, a bluebird, and two toads are dancing and singing the "No Pest" song.
(To the tune of Frere Jacques)
We are hungry,
We are hungry,
Watch out pests,
Watch out pests,
Don't use harmful poisons,

Don't use harmful poisons,
We are best,
We are best.

(They repeat the song as Bugsy crawls on stage.) Kids dressed up as vegetables can be sitting in a garden.

Bugsy: What's going on? Who are you?

Jaws: Look, my friends. It's a juicy little squash bug. Who wants to eat it? (Jaws starts chasing Bugsy around the garden.)

Bugsy: No, no, please don't eat me! I just came from the Joneses' garden to see what's happening here.

Jaws: It's a mess over there. You pests eat all the vegetables and the Joneses don't have much left for themselves.

Bugsy: But I get hungry just like you do.

Wormer: Give him a break, Jaws.

Jaws: OK, OK . . . I'm pretty full myself. You see . . . what's your name again?

Bugsy: I never told you . . .but it's Bugsy.

Jaws: You see, Bugsy, the Bishops got smart. IPM smart.

Wormer: Yeah, they aren't using as many dangerous poisons as they used to. Instead they've put up nesting boxes for me and my other feathered friends. I love to eat caterpillars. (holds up a nesting box)

Warty: So do we, so they made us a toad house.

Jaws: And they brought in praying mantid egg cases and ladybug beetles and let them go in the garden.

Wormer: And they also planted special plants that pests like you don't like to eat.

Hopper: And they even have neighborhood kids come in and pick off pests. The kids get paid and the vegetables don't get eaten.

Wormer: Without poisons, it is safer for everyone—except for pests.

Toads: Yes, it's much safer.

Bugsy: Well, I'm going back to the Joneses' garden—before any of you guys get hungry again. . . .

Jaws: You'd better watch out, Bugsy—I saw Mr. Jones talking to Mrs. Bishop . . .

Wormer: That's right. It won't be long until the Joneses are using Integrated Pest Management too.

(Bugsy walks off the stage with a worried look.)

All the predators gather together and sing the "No Pest" song again.

Insect Time Machine

Find out how insects have influenced people through time.

Objective:
State 3 ways insects have influenced human society.

Ages:
Intermediate and Advanced

Materials:
- *insect reference books*
- *paper and pencils*

Subjects:
History, Social Studies, and Science

Have your group zip back and forth in time with this "Insect Time Machine" activity. They will be able to see the many ways insects have influenced people in the past and how they influence people today.

On slips of paper, write down the names of insects that have had either a positive or negative effect on human society. (See the list below for suggestions. We've used examples from the past and from the present.) Then divide the class into study teams and have each team pick one of the slips out of a "hat." Give each group time in the library to find out about the effects—good, bad, or both—that their particular insect has had on people. (The slips can just have the insect's name or the insect's name and some clues about how the insect has influenced people.)

After each group has had time to look for information, lead a discussion with them. Here are some ideas and questions to talk about as each of the groups tells about its insect:

- Does the insect have the same (negative or positive) impact on us today that it has had in the past? Why or why not?
- How might the insect's role in human society change in the future?
- How does the insect affect other animals?
- In what ways would the world be different if the insect had never existed?

SUGGESTIONS

- fruit fly (use of fruit flies in genetic research, Mediterranean fruit fly attacks on crops)
- gypsy moth (introduced from Europe in 1868, outbreaks in the Northeast, controversial pesticide spraying to control)
- honey bee (producer of honey and wax, great pollinator, killer bee scare)

- ants (spread of the fire ant since its introduction in 1940)
- mosquitoes (malaria, yellow fever, dog heartworm)
- ladybug beetle (biological control: Australian ladybug beetle brought to California in 1888 to control cottony cushion scale)
- tsetse fly (sleeping sickness)
- boll weevil (cotton destroyer)
- fleas (outbreaks of bubonic plague throughout history: ancient Rome, Asia in the 1300s, England in the 1600s, India in early 1900s, etc.)
- silkworm moths (production of silk as far back as 2500 BC)
- bedbugs (once common, some spread diseases)
- lice (outbreaks in livestock and human populations)
- grasshoppers (evidence of locust devastation in ancient civilizations, locust attacks in Mississippi Valley in 1870s, 1921 discovery of why locusts swarm)
- scarab beetles (ancient Egyptian religious symbol, dung beetles brought to Australia to get rid of cow dung)
- butterflies (beauty and design, butterflies in art)
- lac scale (used to make shellac)
- flour beetle (eats grain—is a serious pest in flour mills and other granaries)

SCARAB BEETLE

Grasshopper Goulash and Maggot Muffins

Conduct a survey to find out how people feel about eating insects.

Objectives:
Discuss how people feel about eating insects and using insect foods to supplement their diets. State the food value of insects.

Ages:
Intermediate and Advanced

Materials:
* pencils and paper

Subjects:
Social Studies and Science

It's dinnertime. How about some grasshopper goulash or maggot muffins? As the world's population increases, more and more people are taking a closer look at insects as a food supplement.

Many people around the world already eat insects in great numbers. Some cultures fry or roast grasshoppers. Others dry and grind up beetle grubs and fly maggots into protein flour. And many people eat fat, juicy caterpillars, cooked like french fries.

The idea of eating insects is repulsive to many people. Yet insects are high in protein and available in large numbers—two important factors that make insect foods a practical idea for the future.

To find out how people really feel about eating insects, have your group conduct a survey. Divide the group into teams of 5 and have each team make up its own survey questions. Here are some sample questions:

* Have you ever eaten an insect in any form?
* If not, would you ever consider eating one? Why or why not?
* Do you think insects will ever be accepted as a protein source in North America?
* Would you eat
  —insect protein flakes if they looked and tasted like corn flakes?
  —insect flour if it looked and tasted like wheat flour?
  —grasshopper stew if it tasted like chicken stew?
* We eat other arthropods such as crayfish, lobsters, and crabs. Why don't we eat insects?

After surveying as many people as possible, have each group tally the results and report back to the others. Discuss how your group feels about insect foods of the future and how insects might be able to help fight world hunger. You might also want to hold an insect recipe contest . . . but that's up to you.

Insects in the News

Make a bulletin board about insects in the news.

Objectives:
Name two current events that have to do with insects. Describe ways that insects "make the news."

Ages:
Intermediate and Advanced

Materials:
* newspaper articles
* extra newspapers for background
* colored construction paper
* yarn
* plastic wrap
* scissors

Subjects:
Current Events, Social Studies, and Science

Most of us never think of insects as being big newsmakers. But insects are actually in the news quite a bit. In the past, medflies (Mediterranean fruit flies), gypsy moths, and killer bees have been responsible for some of the more sensational insect news stories. But other aspects of the insect world—their role in scientific research, for example—are newsworthy too. This bulletin board idea will help your group become aware of insect current events and bring them up to date on some aspects of insect research.

HOW TO MAKE A "BUGGY" BULLETIN BOARD

Line your bulletin board with sheets of newspaper. Collect articles, ads, and pictures of insects in the news. (Have the kids help search.) Paste the articles to colored paper and arrange them on the board. Cut out pictures of insects, make little reading glasses for them with yarn and plastic (from bags and wrap), and position them so that it looks as if they're reading the articles.

Insect Trivia

- During a single meal, a female mosquito can drink her own weight in blood.
- Some mayflies live 24 hours or less as adults.
- The smallest insect ever discovered is a hairy-winged beetle from the tropics. It measures 1/100 of an inch (.25 mm) in length.
- The longest insect ever found is a tropical stick insect from Asia. Some of the females get to be over a foot (30 cm) long.
- Over one million different kinds of insects have been discovered. This is twice the total of all other kinds of animals put together.
- A swarm of desert locusts (of the grasshopper family), containing over 1000 million insects, has covered an estimated area of 2000 square miles (5200 km^2). Swarms of locusts have been seen at sea 1200 miles from land (1920 km).
- Bombardier beetles can shoot a hot, smelly liquid from their abdomen that is 212° F (100° C).
- Fireflies aren't the only light-producing insects. Some click beetles, springtails, and gnats also light up.
- There is a fly in California called the petroleum fly that lives and breeds in petroleum.
- The largest animal in Antarctica that lives strictly on land is a wingless fly less than 1/4 of an inch (6 mm) long.
- The color a head louse will be as an adult can depend on the color of the person's hair it is living in. For example, a louse living in blond hair would most likely be a light color; one living in black hair would be dark.
- A cockroach can live nine days without its head.
  - Fleas can jump 200 times the length of their bodies.
  - Some queen termites live as long as 50 years.
  - The atlas moth of India is one of the world's largest insects. It measures 12 inches (30 cm) from wingtip to wingtip.
  - A tiny insect called a biting midge can beat its wings 1000 times a second.

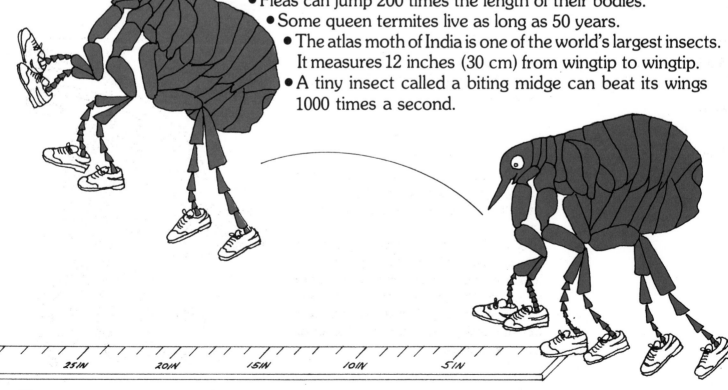

25 IN   20 IN   15 IN   10 IN   5 IN

RANGER RICK'S NATURESCOPE: INCREDIBLE INSECTS

CRAFTY CORNER

Insects are great subjects for exciting art and craft projects. The ideas in this section complement many of the activities in the first five chapters.

Punched-Out Insects

Subject:
Art

Ages:
Primary

Materials:
- *paper punch*
- *plain white typing paper*
- *scraps of colored construction paper*
- *white glue*

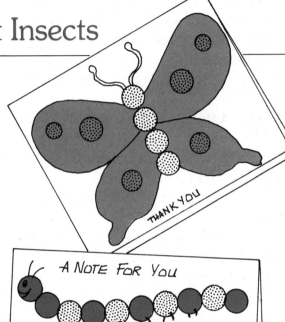

After studying insects, have your kids design their own insect note paper, using bright paper dots.

First punch out dots of colored paper using a hand paper punch. (The brighter the colors the better.) For the stationery, use sheets of plain white typing paper cut in half and folded. (You can use colored construction paper too.)

Have your students glue the dots in the shapes of beetles, butterflies, caterpillars, moths, dragonflies, or other insects to the top, side, or bottom of the folded notepaper. Draw eyes, legs, antennae, and other body parts on with a felt-tipped pen.

Sculpting with Scraps

Subject:
Art

Ages:
Primary

Materials:
- *lids, caps, and bottle tops*
- *pipe cleaners*
- *yarn*
- *glue*

Here is an idea for making fantasy insects by recycling the "junk" we normally throw away.

BOTTLE TOP BUGS

Have your group collect a whole bunch of lids, caps, and tops from milk jugs, toothpaste tubes, pop bottles, and salad dressing jars.

Glue the lids and caps together as illustrated to make interesting insect critters. Let the glue become tacky before attaching. Add pipe cleaners as legs and antennae. To hang the insects on an insect tree or mobile, tie a yarn loop to the top or glue one in place.

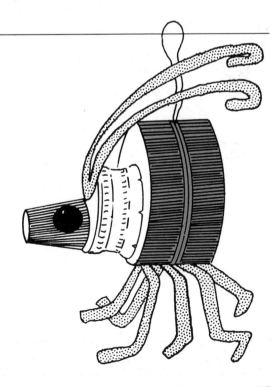

Marvelous Insect Model

Subject:
Art

Ages:
Primary, Intermediate, and Advanced

Materials:
- *long balloon*
- *yarn and thread*
- *white glue*
- *heavy paper*
- *clear plastic wrap*
- *food coloring*
- *paintbrushes*
- *paper fasteners*
- *pipe cleaners*
- *little Styrofoam balls*
- *knife*

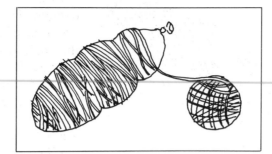

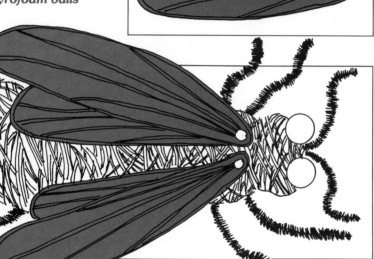

Children will love making their own big hanging insects. It's a creative way to review insect body parts. Here's how to do it:

1. Blow up the balloon most of the way, and then use two pieces of strong thread to tie it into the three insect body sections: head, thorax, and abdomen.
2. Dip the yarn into white glue and wrap it around the balloon in all directions. Let the body dry. Pop and carefully remove the balloon through a crack in the yarn.
3. Draw an outline for two pairs of wings on heavy paper. Cover the paper with clear plastic wrap. Squeeze the glue onto the wrap in a vein pattern. Press pieces of yarn into the glue. Let this dry.
4. Mix white glue with a few drops of food coloring. Paint this all over the wings. Dry the wings, and then carefully peel the wings away from the paper and plastic.
5. Attach the wings to the thorax with paper fasteners. Glue pipe cleaners to the head and thorax for antennae and legs. To make eyes cut a small Styrofoam ball in half and glue each half to the head. (Cut these for the children.)
6. Tie a strong thread to both ends of the marvelous model, and hang it up to fly.

Kooky Caterpillars

Subject:
Art

Ages:
Intermediate and Advanced

Materials:
- *long nylon socks*
- *fiberfill, cotton balls, pantyhose, or other stuffing material*
- *needles and thread*
- *colored yarn*
- *scissors*
- *colored felt scraps*
- *glue*
- *colored pipe cleaners*

Nearly everybody has spare socks lying around whose mates have long since disappeared. Making Kooky Caterpillars is one way to put those spare socks to good use.

Have each child bring in a needle and thread and a nylon sock. (The bigger and stretchier the sock, the better.) Socks with bright colors, stripes, or funny patterns can make some interesting caterpillars—but the less flashy styles will work too. Give the kids enough fiberfill or cotton batting to stuff their socks. (If you don't want to buy these materials, have the kids bring in pantyhose or cloth scraps for stuffing.)

The toe end of each sock will be the caterpillar's head. Tell the kids to stuff extra material into the toe so the head will be larger than the caterpillar's body segments.

Next have them tie off the head segment by wrapping yarn around the sock and tying the two ends of the yarn together. They can stuff and tie off the rest of the segments in the same way. (Excess yarn can either be trimmed off or tucked underneath the rest of the yarn.) When they reach the ends of the socks they can sew them shut or "tie" them off with rubber bands.

Now the kids can cut out and glue on eyes, mouths, and other features from the

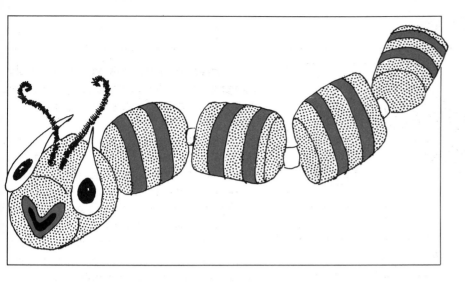

scraps of colored felt. Some may even want to decorate their caterpillars' body segments with felt stripes, dots, and other designs. To add antennae, the kids can use a pencil or pen to poke two holes in their caterpillars' heads. Then have them push a colored pipe cleaner into each hole and add some glue so the antennae will stay put. They can either leave the ends of the pipe cleaners straight or curl them around a pencil.

When all the kids finish, have them place their caterpillars on display around the room. Then take a vote to see whose caterpillar is the kookiest!

Insect Sculptures

Subject:
Art

Ages:
All

Materials:
- *modeling dough (see recipe at right)*
- *arts and crafts scraps*
- *acrylic or tempera paints and brushes*
- *pictures of insects*
- *food coloring (optional)*
- *insect field guides (optional)*

Playing with modeling dough is fun for any age child. In this activity your group can make amazing imaginary insects or realistic ones using homemade modeling dough that hardens.

To make the dough, mix the following ingredients in a saucepan:

> 2 cups flour
> 2 tablespoons oil
> 1 cup salt
> 2 cups water
> 4 teaspoons cream of tartar
> vanilla or peppermint flavoring (to make it smell nice)

Cook over medium heat, stirring until the mixture starts boiling or forms a ball (about 2-3 minutes). Remove from the heat and let cool until it can be handled.

Knead the dough like bread until smooth and supple. To store the dough, keep it in a plastic bag in a cool place. (Makes enough for 6-8 kids.)

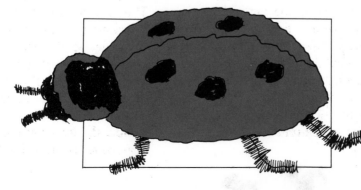

SCULPTING THE INSECT

Before starting, show pictures of adult insects and discuss the characteristics that make insects insects. (See the background on page 4.) Now give each child a lump of modeling dough and put the other materials in piles around the room. Have them roll and mold the dough into a head, thorax, and abdomen. They can use a toothpick to carve lines or dots on the insect's body and make eyes, wings, and legs with dough. You may want to have them try using pipe cleaners or twigs for legs and antennae, wax paper or plastic wrap for wings, and beans for eyes.

With younger kids, try making fantasy insects. Divide the dough into balls and add food coloring to make green, yellow, orange, blue, and red dough. Give each of the children a little lump of each color and let them design their own insects.

Older children can try to make realistic models. Have them each choose an insect to model from a field guide or textbook. Give them white dough and have them mold their insects into shape. When the models are dry (2-3 days), they can paint them with acrylic or tempera paints to resemble the real insects.

APPENDIX

Traps, Nets, and Cages

Materials:
- *large can*
- *ice pick or sharp object to punch holes in the can*
- *bait (honey, molasses, meat, fruit)*
- *screen to cover the bait*
- *petroleum jelly*
- *boxes*
- *white sheet*
- *funnel or coffee cup liner (optional)*
- *plastic container (optional)*

You can catch all kinds of crawling and flying insects by using baited traps. Here are a few traps you can make with your group:

CAN TRAPS

First punch small holes in the bottom of the can so that it won't fill up with water if it rains. Then dig a hole in the ground and sink the can so that its top is at ground level. (Pick a spot that is rich in insect life.)

For bait, you can use a piece of meat left to decay, molasses or honey, or fermented fruit. Put the bait at the bottom of the can and cover the food with a screen. (That way you won't have to pick through the bait to see the insects.)

Experiment with different baits to see which foods attract which kinds of insects. Try setting up cans containing the same bait in several different locations. Which cans attract the most insects?

You can also use plastic coffee cup liners or small plastic funnels in making traps. Put the funnels in a plastic container or can and place bait at the bottom. Insects walking by will slide down the funnel and into the trap. What kinds of creatures crawled in besides insects?

BOX TRAPS

To catch insects such as cockroaches, silverfish, and beetles inside a building, use an open-topped cardboard box or jar. Set it in a dark, secluded place and put the bait inside. (Use molasses or honey, moist dog food, or any leftover bits of food.) Build a ramp up the side of the box onto the top of the box. Then coat the inside upper two or three inches with petroleum jelly. Once insects crawl in to get the bait, they'll have a hard time crawling out.

SUGARIN'

You can also attract insects by using a sweet concoction of fermented fruit juices, stale beer, mushy bananas, and molasses or honey. Mix it all together and spread it on tree trunks, fence posts, stumps, and logs. Beetles, ants, roaches, flies, and butterflies may come to feed. Try this activity during the day and at night to see if you attract different insects. You will probably also attract daddy longlegs, spiders, sowbugs, and maybe even some mammals, amphibians, or reptiles.

THE SHEET TRICK

Many insects have a habit of folding their legs and acting dead when they are disturbed. You can make use of this trick to catch them.

Take a white sheet outside and spread it out under a plant. Try shaking a tree or jarring a weed with a stick. See if any insects fall out onto the white sheet.

MAKING AN INSECT NET

Materials:
- *3-foot (1-m) piece of broom handle*
- *strong tape*
- *wire coat hanger*
- *old lace curtain or nylon net, at least 45 inches (114 cm) long and 24 inches (61 cm) wide*
- *strip of muslin (or other cotton fabric) about 45 inches (114 cm) long and 3 inches (8 cm) wide*

Here's an easy net to make for capturing flying and hopping insects that are hard to catch by hand. (It is not the sturdiest net, but it will work well for beginning collectors.)
1. First straighten the hook on the coat hanger.
2. Bend the rest of the hanger into a circle.
3. Tape the straightened hook very tightly to the broom handle. Wrap the tape around many times to be sure that it will not tear loose.
4. Now measure around the wire circle. (If you don't have a flexible cloth measuring tape,

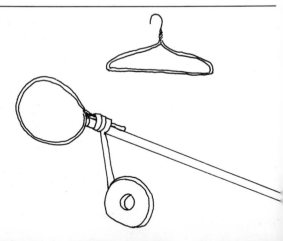

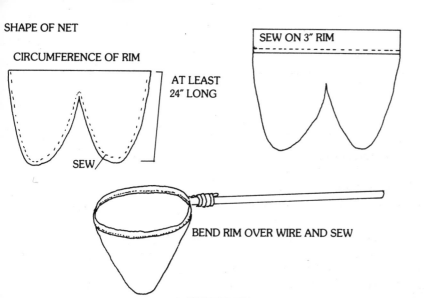

CIRCUMFERENCE OF RIM

SEW ON 3" RIM

AT LEAST 24" LONG

SEW

BEND RIM OVER WIRE AND SEW

you can figure out the circumference by measuring the diameter of the circle and multiplying by 3.14.)

5. Then cut out a piece of net fabric the length of the circumference and shaped as shown (see diagram).
6. Sew the 3-inch-wide fabric to the top edge of the bag. This helps to keep the bag from tearing loose from the wire loop of the net.
7. Sew the side seam shut, leaving the top open.
8. Finish by sewing the bag to the wire loop. (Bend the cotton material over the rim and sew it to itself.)

FLOWERPOT CAGE

Materials:
- *flowerpot*
- *food plant of the insect*
- *cylinder of clear plastic, glass, or screen*
- *gauze*
- *rubber band*

To watch a plant-feeding insect up close, make a "flowerpot" cage. First plant the insect's food plant in a flowerpot or large can. Cover the plant with a cylinder of clear plastic, glass, or screen. The cylinder should be open at both ends. (If you are going to watch for only a short time, you can invert a glass jar over the plant.)

Put the insect on the plant and cover the top with gauze held on by a rubber band.

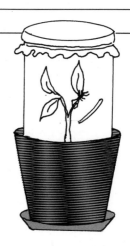

BUILDING A BERLESE FUNNEL

Materials:
- *plastic, metal, or cardboard funnel*
- *screen or wire gauze to fit halfway down the funnel (best if cut in a circle)*
- *stand to support the funnel (cardboard works well)*
- *25-watt light bulb and extension cord*
- *soil sample*
- *plastic bag with a seal*
- *baby food jar and a jelly jar*
- *alcohol (optional)*

Many kinds of tiny insects and other creatures live in the soil and leaf litter on the forest floor. Your kids will be surprised at all the hopping and crawling that goes on there all year, even in areas that get snow. To get a closeup look, try making a Berlese funnel (named for the scientist who invented it).

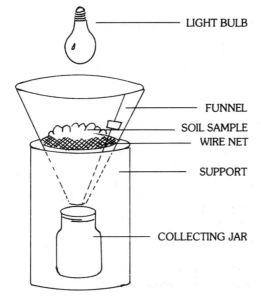

LIGHT BULB

FUNNEL

SOIL SAMPLE

WIRE NET

SUPPORT

COLLECTING JAR

First scoop up a large sample of leaf litter and topsoil and put it in a plastic bag or collecting sack. Try to get moist soil and damp leaves, because soil creatures need to stay damp.

Set up your Berlese funnel as follows:
1. Make a support stand for the funnel by bending fairly stiff cardboard into a cylinder.
2. Cut the mesh screen in a circle so it rests inside the funnel.
3. Set the collecting cup (jelly jar) on the floor so that it will be under the funnel. (If you want to preserve the insects and other creatures, fill the collecting cup with 70% ethyl alcohol or isopropyl (rubbing) alcohol.)
4. Now place your soil sample carefully on the mesh screen in the funnel. Hang a 25-watt light bulb over the sample (see the diagram).
5. Switch on the light and leave it on for several hours. The heat from the light bulb will drive most of the creatures down through the soil and eventually cause them to fall through the screen and into the collecting cup under the funnel.
6. Put the animals you catch in baby food jars of alcohol to examine them closely.

Questions, Questions, and More Questions

1. How many main body parts does an insect have? (3)
2. What are the 3 main body parts of an insect? (head, thorax, and abdomen)
3. Insects are arthropods. What other animals are arthropods? (crabs, lobsters, crayfish, spiders, centipedes, ticks, mites, and millipedes)
4. Give 2 characteristics of arthropods. (exoskeleton, segmented bodies, jointed appendages)
5. How many legs do most insects have? (Most adults have 6; some larvae have none.)
6. Name 2 ways insects are different from spiders. (Spiders have 2 body divisions, 8 legs, no wings, simple eyes, and no antennae; insects have 3 body divisions, 6 legs, 2 antennae, compound and simple eyes, and wings.)
7. Describe 2 types of insect mouths. (chewing, sucking, piercing-sucking, lapping)
8. Which insects have sucking-tube mouths? (moths and butterflies)
9. What is an insect exoskeleton? (hard outer shell)
10. What happens to an insect's hard exoskeleton as the insect grows? (The insect sheds, or "molts," its exoskeleton.)
11. List 3 things an insect can use its legs for. (walking, jumping, swimming, climbing, making noise, catching prey, crawling)
12. What is a compound eye made up of? (many tiny lenses)
13. What do insects use their antennae for? (feeling, smelling, hearing, tasting)
14. Do insects breathe through lungs? (No, they breathe through tracheae.)
15. Do insects have blood? (yes)
16. What is metamorphosis? (the changes in form an insect goes through as it grows)
17. What are the stages of complete metamorphosis? (egg—larva—pupa—adult)
18. What are the stages of incomplete, or simple, metamorphosis? (egg—nymph—adult)
19. What are 2 good things insects do for people? (Provide honey, shellac, silk; pollinate crops; become tools for research; control insect pests; break down dead materials.)
20. What are 2 reasons people don't like insects? (feed on crops, spread human diseases, sting and bite)
21. What is Integrated Pest Management? (A new way of controlling insect pests by combining many methods.)
22. Name 3 things that can be used to control insect pests. (habitat changes, pesticides, sterile insects, natural predators, parasites, hormones, mixed plantings)
23. Name 2 insect pests. (cockroach, mosquito, house fly, weevil, termite)
24. Name 2 beneficial insects. (ladybug beetle, praying mantid, honey bee)
25. Are all insects bugs? (No, bugs are only one group of insects.)
26. What is camouflage? (a means of blending in with the surroundings)
27. What is a cocoon? (a silk case spun by a moth larva when it is ready to pupate)
28. Do any insects live in the soil? (yes)
29. What is a gall? (swelling in a plant where an insect has laid an egg or eggs)
30. What is a caterpillar? (larva of a butterfly or moth)
31. What is a maggot? (larva of a fly)
32. What is a grub? (larva of a beetle)
33. Name an insect that lives in a colony or hive. (termite, bee, wasp, ant)
34. What do aphids eat? (plant juices)
35. What do praying mantids eat? (other insects)
36. Name 3 things that all insects need in order to survive. (food, water, shelter, a place to lay their eggs, the right temperature and humidity)
37. What do most butterflies eat? (nectar from flowers)
38. What is an entomologist? (a scientist who studies insects)
39. List 3 reasons that insects are so successful as an animal group. (small size, high rate of reproduction, large number of offspring, ability to fly)
40. List 3 places an insect might live. (almost anywhere—your house, a tree, the soil, a pond . . . but rarely the ocean)
41. What is a spiracle? (tiny opening in the exoskeleton through which an insect gets oxygen from the air)
42. Name 2 insects that may live in your schoolyard. (Answer depends on locale.)
43. What do insects do in the winter? (Some hibernate as eggs, larvae, pupae, or adults; some remain active; some migrate to other areas.)
44. What is a larva? (the young of an insect that goes through complete metamorphosis)
45. What is a nymph? (the young of an insect that goes through incomplete metamorphosis)

Insect Glossary

abdomen—the last of an insect's 3 main body parts.

adapt—change to fit the environment. For example, back-swimmers have adapted to living in water by having oar-like hind legs.

antennae (singular: antenna)—sensory organs on an insect's head. Antennae are used to smell, taste, feel, and sometimes hear.

arthropods—a group of animals that have exoskeletons, jointed legs, and segmented bodies (phylum: *Arthropoda*). Arthropods include such animals as insects, spiders, ticks, centipedes, millipedes, crayfish, lobsters, mites, and scorpions.

biological control—using natural means to control insect pests. Biological controls are used as an alternative to spraying poisons and using harmful chemicals to control insects. Examples include using natural predators to control insect pests, such as introducing ladybug beetles into your garden to eat the aphids.

camouflage—a means of blending in with the surroundings. For example, walking sticks are camouflaged in trees because they blend in with the green leaves and brown twigs.

chrysalis—pupal case of many butterflies.

cold-blooded—not able to maintain a constant body temperature independent of the outside temperature. Insects, reptiles, fish, and amphibians are cold-blooded.

compound eyes—eyes made up of many tiny units. Each unit has a separate lens, is shaped like a hexagon, and is connected to special cells underneath. With compound eyes, an insect sees a mosaic picture of the world around it. Dragonflies, which have very large compound eyes, have over 25,000 units making up each eye.

cocoon—pupal case of many moths, made out of silk.

entomologist—a scientist who studies insects.

entomology—the study of insects.

exoskeleton—a hard, protective covering found on insects, spiders, and other arthropods. The outer "skeleton."

habitat—the type of environment in which an animal or plant lives. For example, the habitat of a grasshopper is often a field or grassy backyard.

head—the first of an insect's 3 main body parts. An insect's eyes, mouth, and antennae are always found on the head.

IPM—Integrated Pest Management—a way of controlling insect pests using a variety of methods in the best combination. Methods include biological control, habitat changes, and the use of chemicals.

larva (plural: larvae)—the immature stage of an insect that goes through complete metamorphosis (i.e., egg—larva—pupa—adult). Insect larvae look very different from the adults they will become. For example, moth or butterfly larvae are caterpillars, fly larvae are maggots, and beetle larvae are grubs.

mandibles—the outer mouthparts, or jaws, of an insect. Easiest to see in chewing insects, such as grasshoppers, crickets, and beetles. The mandibles, or jaws, move sideways and can cut, grind, and grab.

metamorphosis—the change of an insect (or other animal) from one form to another as it develops into an adult. Some insects go through a 3-stage life cycle called incomplete or simple metamorphosis: egg—nymph—adult. Others go through a 4-stage complete metamorphosis: egg—larva—pupa—adult.

molt—to shed the exoskeleton or outer skin. As an insect grows, it molts several times before it reaches the adult stage.

nymph—the immature stage of an insect that goes through incomplete or simple metamorphosis. It often looks and acts much like an adult, but has no wings and is smaller.

pupa (plural: pupae)—the resting or inactive stage of an insect that goes through complete metamorphosis. The larva changes into a pupa, and then the pupa becomes an adult.

spider—an arthropod that has 2 main body parts, 4 pairs of legs, fangs, and several (often 8) simple eyes. Spiders are closely related to insects.

spiracles—tiny holes in the exoskeleton through which insects breathe.

thorax—the middle of an insect's 3 body parts. The legs and wings are attached to it.

tracheae—tiny tubes that carry oxygen. The tracheae connect to the spiracles.

warm-blooded—able to maintain a constant body temperature independent of the outside temperature. Birds and mammals are warm-blooded.

1998 UPDATE

TABLE OF CONTENTS

WHAT INSECT IS IT? 63

BUG-EYED 66

WHAT A WAY TO GROW 69

MOVE IT! 71

SCARE TACTICS 72

LAND OF THE GIANT INSECTS 73

LAND AND WATER INSECTS 75

COPYCAT PAGES 76
• What Insect Is It?
• Bug-Eyed
• What a Way to Grow
• Move It!
• Scare Tactics
• Land of the Giant Insects
• Land and Water Insects

INSECTS BIBLIOGRAPHY 92

ANSWERS TO COPYCAT PAGES 94

WHAT INSECT IS IT?

Make an insect field guide to help identify different kinds of insects.

Objectives:
Learn how to recognize and distinguish one kind of insect from another. Fill in field guide entries about insects students are most likely to find where they live.

Ages:
All

Materials:
- *Copies of pages 76, 77, and 78*
- *Scissors*
- *Stapler*
- *Crayons, markers*

Subjects:
Science and Art

S ome insects sting. Others bite. Still others destroy crops and garden plants. These are just a few of the reasons why it is important to be able to identify one insect species from another. The field guide exercise emphasizes the observation skills involved in the process of identification, written or pictoral means of description, and the information such identification provides. For instance, the way an insect looks can offer clues to its habitat, on what it may feed, how it may escape danger, and if it may be related to one or more other species.

Challenge your kids to make a list of how they tell one kind of animal from another (shape, size, colors, numbers of legs, etc.). How would they know an insect if they came across it in their backyards or in the park? (See "What Makes An Insect An Insect" on page 4.)

Bring in a field guide to insects and pass it around the room. If you don't own one, most likely there is a copy in the library. Select one of the pictures and ask a few students to describe what they see. Then read that insect's entry stressing the kinds of information such a guide provides (description, food, habitat, etc.). Can students figure out why people turn to field guides to help them identify insects? (There are so many insect species that look similar it is difficult to tell them apart. Having a picture for quick reference as well as facts such as size and color help make on-the-spot identification easier especially when an insect

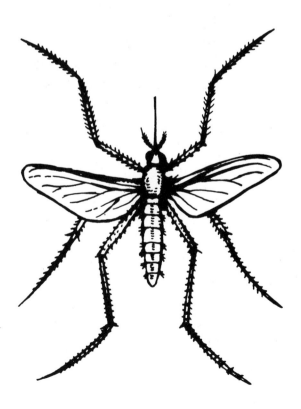

is busy feeding or flying and may be gone in seconds.)

Photocopy pages 76, 77, and 78 and invite students to make their own field guides. Seven insects are pictured. Have students read the text below each. Four entries are blank. Have they seen any of these insects? Have they seen similar insects? Encourage students to draw pictures of insects they have seen or paste down pictures they find in newspapers or magazines. Students should then fill in the entry lines below their pictures with information they already know about the insects, or they can use the field guide to obtain it. Kids should use the text already in their guides as a model for the kinds of information they might have in their entries. They may also want to

look for another ant species and compare it to the Little Black Ant. Or they may choose a moth and want to compare it to the Swallowtail Butterfly. They may want to create a field guide containing only local insects. That would be great, too. Ask students to read their entries to the class. Students may want to refer to the field guide to color all the insects in the guides they make.

Making the Field Guide

1. Fold each page in half along the middle solid line then in half again so the printed sides are on the outside.
2. Nest the three folded pages together so that the numbers are in order from the cover to 12. Pages 6 and 7 should be in the center. Pages 8 to 12 have neither pictures nor printed text.

3. Staple the folded sheets in the middle as shown:

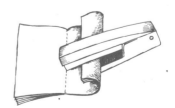

BUG-EYED

Make a model of an insect's compound eye.

Objectives:
Understand the multi-lens structure of an insect's compound eye. Compare what an insect "sees" to what a human does.

Ages:
All

Materials:
- *Copies of pages 79 and 80*
- *Scissors*

Subject:
Science

Ask your kids whether they think all animals with eyes see the world the same way they do. Ask the kids who answer yes whether they think humans can see as well at night as owls, for instance. List their reasons on the board.

Now challenge kids to brainstorm what insects need to see in order to stay alive (where food is, where danger lurks, the way to escape predators, how to fly without hitting anything, etc.). Have they ever watched an insect fly from flower to flower? If so have them describe what the insect did. Have they ever tried to swat a mosquito or a fly? Do they think the insect saw the danger as it flew to safety?

At one time or another some students may have gotten a close-up look at the eyes of a fly or a dragonfly. If so, have invite them to make a rough sketch on the board of what they remember about the eyes. Were

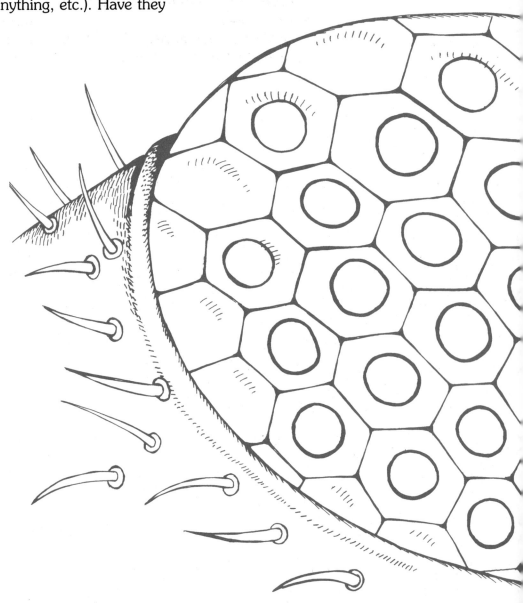

the eyes flat or did they bulge? How did the insect eyes compare with theirs? If they had eyes proportionally as large on their head, how big do they think such bulging eyes would be?

Explain that many insects have two kinds of eyes. The two big "bug eyes" the kids may remember are called compound eyes. But many insects also have one to three simple eyes called *ocelli*. While these simple eyes can sense light from darkness, it is the compound eyes that allow insects to see images.

Hold up a copy of page 79 and tell the kids that it shows the outside of one compound eye. What does it remind them of (a honeycomb, kernels on an ear of corn, etc.)? Explain that each six-sided unit is the outer part of an *ommatidium*. Point to the ommatidium at the right of the eye. The outer part is transparent so light can get it. It also acts as a lens that bends and focuses the light down inside the ommatidium. There the light is absorbed by special cells that send signals to the insect's brain.

Remind kids that each of their eyes has only one lens. Students who wear glasses may point out that they need an extra lens over each eye to focus light so they can see clearly.

Divide the class into pairs or groups of three. Have each group select one member to cut out the shape on page 80 without showing it to the others. Be sure to follow the dark black cut line around the PULL LEFT tab. Hand out page 79 to the others in each group. They are to cut out all of the little round CUT OUT holes (one per each ommatidium) as well as the two slits marked CUT HERE. Have them hand this page to the group member holding page 80. That member should place cut out page 80 behind page 79 and insert the two pull tabs into the cut open slits. Pull the right tab so that all of the cut-open holes on the eye are blank. Now turn the model so it faces the other group members and slowly pull the other tab to the left. What do the other members see first—an image or just something moving across the ommatidia? Can they figure out what the insect is looking at? (A butterfly on top of small flowers.)

Explain that no one knows for sure what an insect sees. Unlike a human eye, a compound eye cannot move. Each six-sided ommatidium points in its own direction and sees only a part of what the insect looks at, instead of seeing the entire picture as a human eye does. The insect's brain must put together all of the images coming from all the ommatidia to figure out what the insect is seeing. Have the kids think of each image from an ommatidium as a puzzle piece. All the pieces must be joined together to form the entire picture.

Ask the kids if they had an easy time making out the butterfly. It was probably difficult because the image is broken up by the ommatidia. But an insect may not need to see the world with the same clarity or detail that people do. All of the ommatidia are looking at different directions at the same time. This enables them to pick up movement that signals possible danger nearby. Have the kids ever been in a store which had twenty or more TV sets all tuned to the same channel? What was it like looking at all the sets (lots of movement)? Even the slightest movement appears multiplied many times. In the same way all of the ommatidia may multiply movements so insects can stay alive.

Not all insects have the same number of ommatidia. The more an insect has the better it can see. Dragonflies have more than 10,000 ommatidia per compound eye. Why do kids think these insects need so many? (Dragonflies are swift fliers that catch other insects in mid-air to eat.) Why do kids think cave dwelling insects have none? (In the total darkness of a cave eyes are of no use.)

Kids may be interested in reporting on which colors insects can and cannot see which colors flowering plants depend on to attract insects that help them pollinate and how bees can tell where the sun is even on a cloudy day.

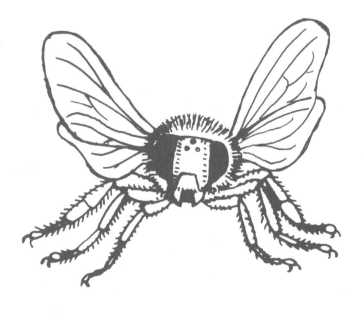

WHAT A WAY TO GROW

*Solve mazes to learn
the growth stages of
complete and incom-
plete metamorphosis.*

Objective:
*Understand the differ-
ence between com-
plete and incomplete
metamorphosis.*

Ages:
All

Materials:
- *Copies of pages 81
  and 82*
- *Scissors*
- *Tape or glue*
- *Pencils or pens*

Subject:
Science

Ask your kids how they have changed in physical appearance since birth. In what ways did they resemble their parents when they were born? (Eye color, hair color, features that made grandparents say "Oh, you look just like . . .") In what ways were you different from your parents? How do your kids expect to change as they grow and develop?

Do any of your kids have pets? Can they describe how those pets have changed in physical appearance since they got them? Do the kids think that their pets looked the same at birth as they do now, only smaller?

Challenge kids to think of an animal that doesn't look at all like its parents during the first part of its life. If students can't think of any, ask if they have ever seen a caterpillar. What does it grow into?—a butterfly or a moth.

All of the changes a living thing goes through during its life make up its life cycle. Invite students to list the stages of a human life cycle: birth, baby, child, teenager, young adult, adult, old age, death. Can kids figure out the stages a rose goes through (seed, seedling, leafy plant, flowering plant)?

Insects, too, go through changes during their life cycles. Some, such as grasshoppers, hatch from their eggs looking like their parents in miniature. They are called nymphs; and they eat, grow, and shed their skin from a few to many times. When the last shed, or molt, takes place, the nymphs develop wings and sex organs. Then they are adults. These stages—egg to nymph to adult—form a life cycle of incomplete metamorphosis (to change shape). For other kinds of insects with similar life cycles, see Growing Up on page 18.

Butterflies go through complete

metamorphosis. They hatch from their eggs as caterpillars. A caterpillar is a larva—a young animal that does not at all resemble its parents. Caterpillars eat, grow, and molt over and over. After the final molt, a hard case called a chrysalis forms around

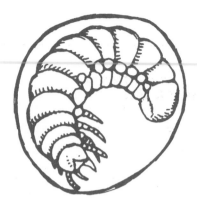

the body of a butterfly caterpillar. The caterpillar now enters the stage when it is a pupa. Inside the crysalis the pupa changes into an adult butterfly which breaks out of its case and flies off to feed and mate. Such a four-stage life cycle—egg to larva to pupa to adult—is called complete metamorphosis. See page 18 for a list of other insects with similar life cycles.

Copy and hand out pages 81 and 82. On them kids will find four life cycle mazes: that of a stag beetle, a mosquito, a shield bug, and a Cecropia moth.

Invite kids to solve each maze. Whenever they come to a circle in the maze, including Start, they should look at the pictures next to all four mazes and select the picture that belongs in that circle. The pictures are labeled with just the animal names so kids have to decide which are the eggs, larvas, adults, etc. They should cut out each picture and tape or glue it in its place then continue with the maze. At the end ask kids which life cycle mazes show incomplete metamorphosis (shield bug) and which show complete (stag beetle,

mosquito, and moth). How can they tell?

Challenge kids to compare the life cycles. How are the larvas alike and different? How do they differ from the adults (size, shape, lack of wings, many legs, etc.)? How do they differ from the shield bug nymph?

Be sure to point out that during their pupal stage, moths don't form a chrysalis but spin a case out of silk. Do kids know what that case is called (a cocoon)? Encourage your kids to find out more about each of the insects in their mazes and report back to the class. For instance, caterpillar have many legs, no wings, simple eyes and chewing mouthparts, while adult butterflies have six legs, wings, compound eyes, and tubelike mouthparts for sipping flower nectar.

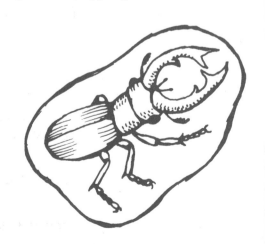

MOVE IT!

Compare the different ways that insects move.

Objectives:
Figure out the ways insects can move and which body parts they use. Compare the body parts to those of other animals that move the same.

Ages:
Primary

Materials:
- *Copy of page 83*
- *Pencil or pen*

Subject:
Science

Invite kids to make a list of all the ways they can move, such as running, jumping, swimming, walking, climbing, crawling, etc. Challenge them to list which parts of their body are most important in making each movement. (For instance, legs for jumping, arms and legs for swimming, etc.) Can kids name other animals that perform some or all of the same movements? What about animals that can move in ways that humans cannot, such as flying? Which body parts do those animals have but humans lack?

Now focus on insects. Which do kids know walk? Fly? Climb, etc.? Hand out copies of page 83. There are six insects in the first column, six words in the second, and six bony animals in the third. Challenge kids to draw a line from each insect to the word that describes its main way of moving then continue each line by matching the same word to the movement of a bony animal.

Ask kids to zero in on each pair of animals connected by the lines. Take the grasshopper and the kangaroo for one. Which body parts do they both use for jumping (their legs with powerful muscles.)? Have kids circle the legs on both of these jumpers then circle the parts on the other pairs they think are most important to the movement.

Divide the class into groups and ask each to find out more about insect movements. Pose questions like these for flying: Do insects fly like birds do? Do all insects have the same number of wings? Can any insects hover in the air or fly backward? What makes butterfly and moth wings so colorful? Which insect has the largest wingspan? How many times a minute does a housefly or a bee flap its wings?

For walking and running, you might ask: How many of their legs do insects lift at a time when walking? How does a fly cling to a ceiling? How do some insects walk on ponds without getting their feet wet? Encourage kids to draw pictures of the insects they mention in their reports. Even better, have them make flash cards of the insects for others in the class to look at and figure out what kinds of movements each insect might make.

ANSWERS

GRASSHOPPER AND KANGAROO: powerful jumping legs

WHIRLIGIG BEETLE AND PLATYPUS: paddlelike legs for swimming

MOLE CRICKET AND MOLE: shovel-shaped legs for digging

FLY AND GECKO LIZARD: legs with suction pads for climbing and clinging

MOTH AND DUCK: wings for flying

TIGER BEETLE AND HORSE: long, strong legs for running

SCARE TACTICS

Objectives:
Understand how false eye spots can mean the difference between life and death. Discuss how some insects can fool predators into not attacking them.

Ages:
Primary

Materials:
- *Copies of page 84*
- *Pencil or pen*

Subject:
Science

The animal world is a tough place in which to stay alive. At every turn a predator may lurk, hungry to make a meal of some other creature. This danger especially pertains to insects because they are food for so many animals, including other insects.

Challenge kids to come up with ways animals defend themselves against attack. List them all—by biting, clawing, running away at full speed, fighting, etc. Ask how a bee would defend itself? Then list for kids some other kinds of insect defenses. (Bombadier beetles squirt hot chemicals at attackers, stink bugs release foul odors and ants spray acid.) All such defenses come into play when a predator is close by. But many insects employ scare tactics that aim at keeping would-be predators as far away as possible.

Hand out page 84 and invite kids first to connect the dots on the top half of the page. Ask them to describe what they see (a moth on a leaf). Before kids connect the dots on the lower half, tell them that the moth senses danger. Can the kids figure out by connecting the dots how the moth deters predators simply by opening its wings? The open wings reveal a pattern that looks like two large eyes on a big animal such as an owl or a snake. Few moth eaters would risk attacking an owl or a snake that might wind up eating them. Instead they pass up the moth with the false eye spots and search for other prey.

Bring in pictures of other insects that illustrate other ways in which they trick predators. Most books show how insects camouflage themselves by making use of their body patterns, colors, and shapes. A perfect example is a walking stick insect. Look, also, for shots of caterpillars that resemble animal droppings, treehoppers that double for thorns, and butterflies easy to mistake for fallen leaves.

Most books on insects contain pictures of the monarch and the viceroy butterfly. Hold these up and ask kids if they can tell the two butterflies apart. (Neither can most butterfly eaters.) Point to the monarch and explain that it has a body poison that makes predators vomit and can kill them if they don't spit the monarch out. When such predators spot the monarch's warning colors, they stay away. Point to the viceroy and tell kids that it is not poisonous, then challenge them to figure out how looking like a monarch helps a viceroy stay alive. (Predators that mistake a viceroy for a monarch will leave it alone.)

Encourage kids to make a poster of all the ways insects warn, trick, and fend off predators. Use photos or let kids draw their own pictures of insects doing the work of staying alive.

LAND OF THE GIANT INSECTS

Make a model of a giant dragonfly that lived about 300 million years ago.

Objectives:
Learn about giant insects that lived in prehistoric times. Infer that even though such insects are extinct similar kinds of insects are still found on Earth.

Ages:
Primary and Intermediate

Materials:
- *Copies of pages 85, 86, 87 and 88*
- *Ruler*
- *Scissors*
- *Tape or glue*
- *Crayons, markers*

Subjects:
Science, Math, Art

I f your kids have seen any movies at all, there is a good chance that one or more has been about the creatures that roamed the Earth from the time of the first dinosaurs until the end of the last Ice Age. Tap into what kids remember by asking them what they know about dinosaurs, woolly mammoths, and other prehistoric life. Most likely kids will wind up describing giant reptiles or mammals that died out millions of years ago. However, some kids may have seen science fiction thrillers about giant flies, or cockroaches, or other insects. The concept of creatures much bigger than those alive today is the perfect lead-in to a time when Earth really was home to some giant insects.

Hand out pages 86, 87, and 88. Invite kids to make the giant dragonfly model. (See the next page for instructions.) Explain that the model is life size. About 300 million years ago such a dragonfly lived in swamps and hunted other insects to eat. There were no trees back then, nor any flowers. Instead, towering horsetails, ferns, and club mosses grew in the swamps. The giant dragonfly was not the only giant animal that lived in these ancient habitats. There were centipedes as long as a kid's arm, millipedes the length of a sleeping bag, and giant amphibians the size of a van. (Note: centipedes and millipedes are arthropods but not insects.) There were cockroaches larger than your hand. Hopefully no such roaches roam your

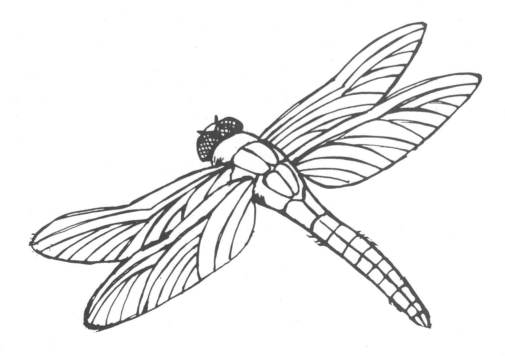

school, but some that size crawl the rainforests of South America.

Hand out page 85 and let kids color their ancient swamp scene. Challenge them to pick out other insects in the picture. (They are the creatures with six legs.) Have kids set their dragonfly model in front of the scene and measure its wingspan with a ruler. If a dragonfly darting around a pond in your local park has a wingspan of about 4 inches, see if your kids can figure out how much bigger the span of the ancient dragonfly's wings was.

Kids may wonder how anyone even knows about giant dragonflies if none exist today. The answer is through fossils—anything that remains of plants and animals that lived a very long time ago. Fossils is a topic perfect for kids to research. Kids may be able to explain how teeth, bones, and shells can remain after millions of years and about insects trapped in amber which was central to the plot of *Jurassic Park*. But do they know about insect outlines pressed into rocks? Divide the class into groups and challenge each group to find out all they can about fossils in general and insect fossils in particular.

MAKING THE DRAGONFLY

1. Hand out one copy of page 86 and two copies of pages 87 and 88.
2. Color all the parts of the dragonfly.
3. Cut out the two pieces on page 86 and tape or glue together as shown:

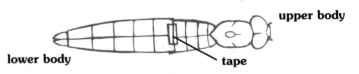

4. Cut out the two RIGHT WING pieces on page 87. Tape the pieces together as shown:

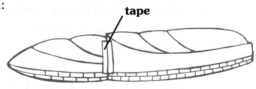

5. Repeat for the other right wing.
6. Tape or glue the front and back right wings to the main body along the TAPE HERE lines as shown:

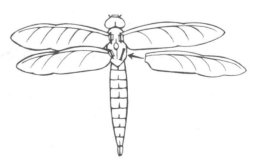

7. Repeat for the left wings.

Land and Water Insects

Use dioramas to compare backyard and pond insects.

Objectives:
Understand how land and water insects are adapted to live where they do. Identify backyard and pond insects.

Ages:
Intermediate

Materials:
- *Copies of pages 84, 85, and 86*
- *Scissors*
- *Tape or glue*
- *Crayons or markers*

Subjects:
Science, Art, Writing Skills

Often half the fun of discovering something new is telling friends and family about it. Especially when that something is as close as the backyard or the pond in the park.

Ask kids what kinds of insects they have seen in their backyard or in the park. What were the insects doing? How could kids tell? Where were the animals—in, on, above the water, on plants, etc.?

Invite kids to make the back-to-back dioramas of backyard and pond (see below for instructions). Their job is to find out about the insects in each habitat and compare what it takes for those insects to stay alive in each.

Divide the class into groups and challenge the kids to research one or two facts about each insect in the backyard and pond dioramas. Facts can include what insects eat, how they breathe, where they lay eggs, how they change during their lives, how they protect themselves from predators, where to look for them (in, on, above the water), how they walk on water without getting their feet wet, what is inside an anthill, etc.

Kids can use this book or field guides to research this information as well as any of the books listed on pages 92 and 93. Kids should choose from all the facts they collect and write a sign to sit in front of each diorama that explains what is going on in the picture. Invite kids to create their own dioramas by drawing pictures of insects they have seen in their own backyard or at a pond.

MAKING THE DIORAMAS

1. Color all the pictures.
2. Fold page 90 in half so the printed sides face out.
3. On page 89 cut out the front piece to the backyard, the Monarch butterfly, the walkingstick, and the backyard sign.
4. Attach the left side of the front piece to the backyard scene as shown.

5. Attach the right side as shown:

6. Tape or glue the butterfly and walkingstick to the front piece or the main picture wherever they like.
7. Fill in the sign piece.
8. Fold and tape the sign as shown:

9. Turn the diorama around and repeat for the pond scene. Tape or glue the red-eared slider and the water strider wherever kids like.

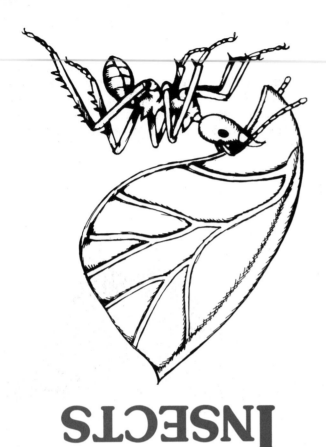

INSECTS

1

12

2

11

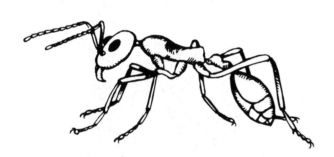

LITTLE BLACK ANT

The shiny little black ant grows about 0.1 inches (0.25 cm) long. Look for it in the park, in the garden, even in your house. See if its carrying food back to its underground nest. Perhaps the ant found a speck of sweet food someone dropped.

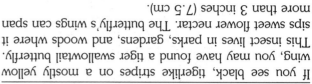

LIGHTNING BUG

Lightning bugs, or fireflies, are really beetles that flash yellow or green light on summer nights. The flashing light helps them attract mates. Some female lightning bugs have no wings. You may know them as glowworms. Lightning bugs grow around 0.5 inches (1.2 cm) long.

TIGER SWALLOWTAIL BUTTERFLY

If you see black, tigerlike stripes on a mostly yellow wing, you may have found a tiger swallowtail butterfly. This insect lives in parks, gardens, and woods where it sips sweet flower nectar. The butterfly's wings can span more than 3 inches (7.5 cm).

8

fold line

fold line

7

FIELD CRICKET

When you hear a field cricket's chirping song, try to figure out where the sound is coming from. To 'sing' an inch- (2.5 cm-) long male cricket rubs his front wings together. The female listens with the eardrum on her leg. Field crickets feed mostly on plants.

BUMBLE BEE

Do you know what "busy as a bee" means? Watch a bumble bee fly from flower to flower and you will find out. As the bee feeds it picks up pollen and carries it to other flowers of the same kind. This helps the flowers form seeds. Black and yellow bumble bees can grow an inch (2.5 cm) long.

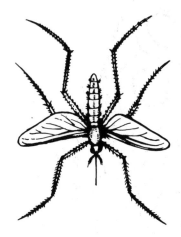

3

MOSQUITO

When a mosquito bites you, don't blame the male. It was the buzzing female in need of blood for her eggs. Rafts of mosquito eggs float in ponds before hatching into wrigglers. These will change into adults that grow about 0.25 inches (0.63 cm) long. Some mosquitoes' bites carry disease but not this kind of mosquito.

fold line

fold line

01

4

9

LADYBIRD BEETLE

About 0.25 inches (0.63 cm) long, this insect is also called a ladybug. Either way, you can tell this beetle by its roundish body and by its spots. Count them, if you can, on the red or orange wing covers. In meadows, marshes, and gardens, ladybird beetles feast on aphids which can damage plants.

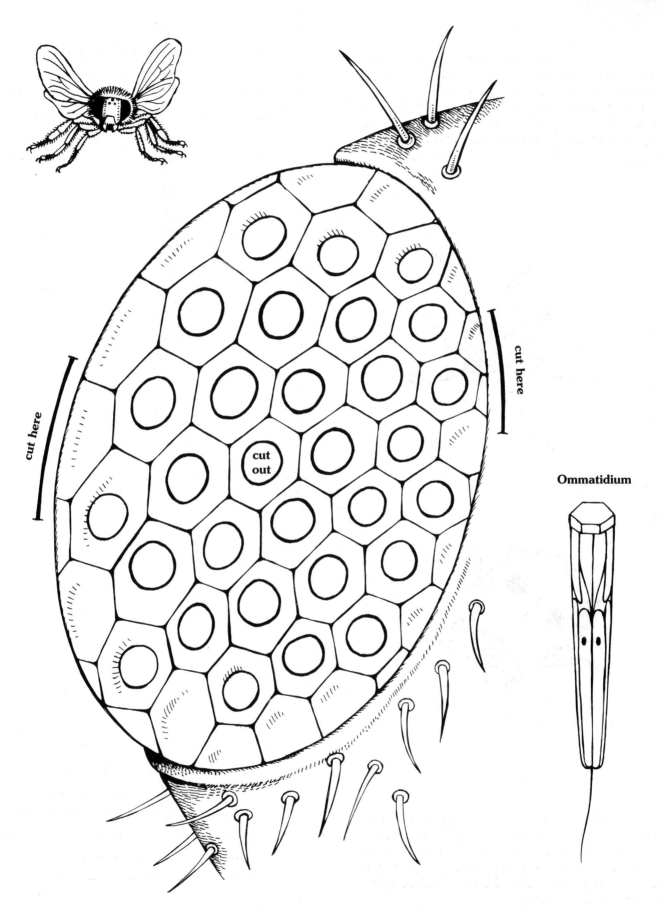

Ommatidium

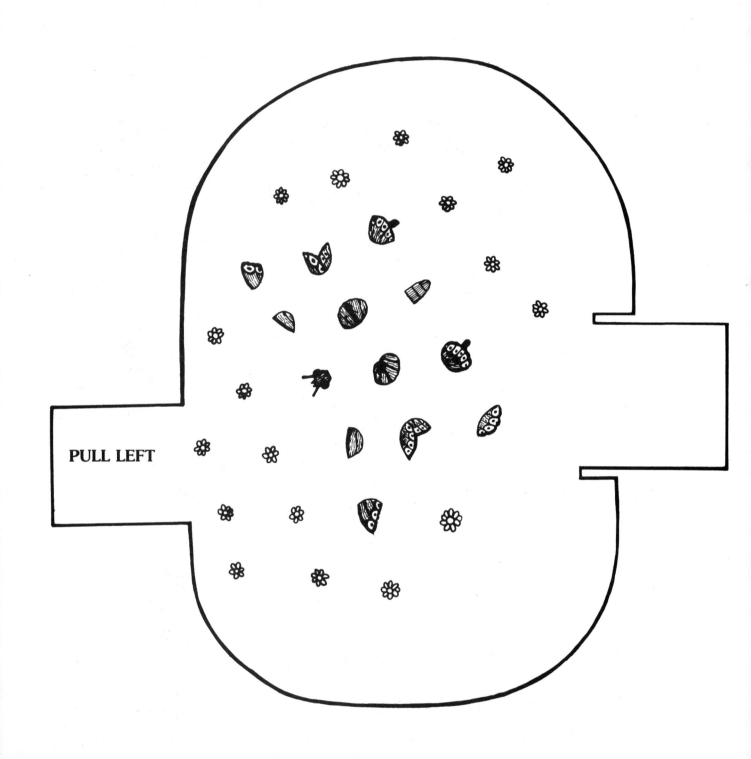

PULL LEFT

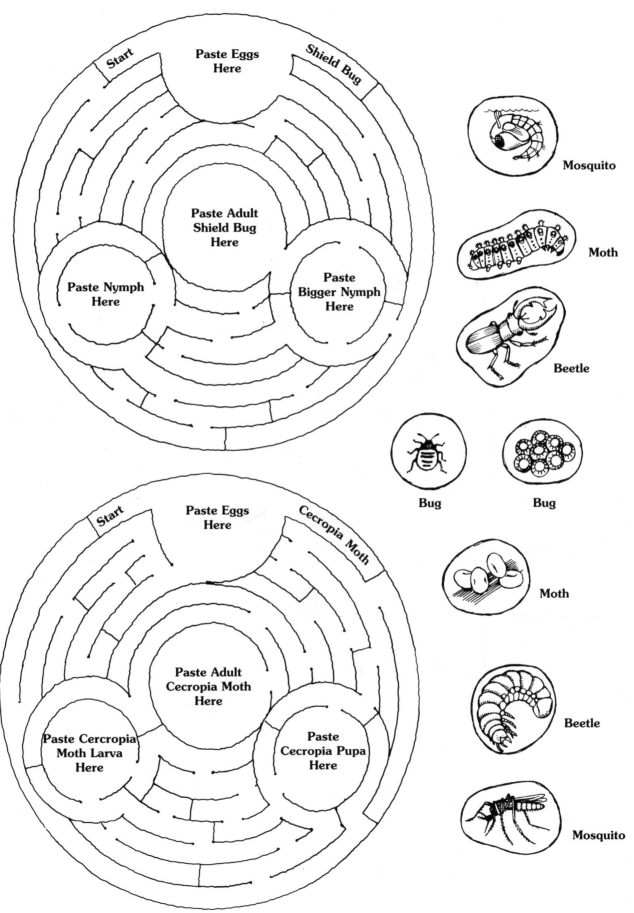

Start

Paste Eggs Here

Shield Bug

Paste Adult Shield Bug Here

Paste Nymph Here

Paste Bigger Nymph Here

Mosquito

Moth

Beetle

Bug

Bug

Moth

Beetle

Mosquito

Start

Paste Eggs Here

Cecropia Moth

Paste Adult Cecropia Moth Here

Paste Cercropia Moth Larva Here

Paste Cecropia Pupa Here

WHAT A WAY TO GROW

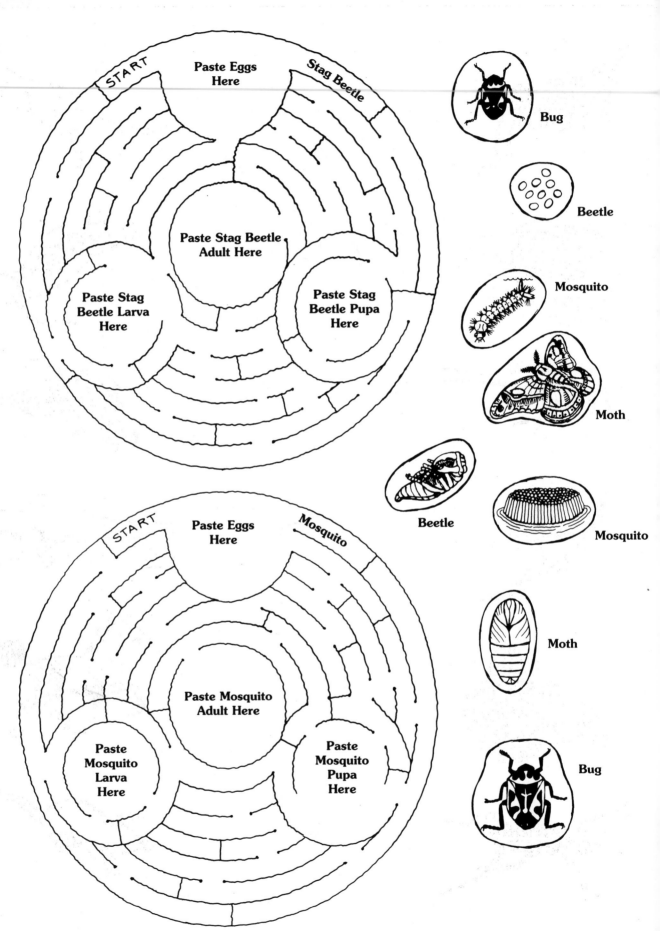

START

Paste Eggs
Here

Stag Beetle

Paste Stag Beetle
Adult Here

Paste Stag
Beetle Larva
Here

Paste Stag
Beetle Pupa
Here

Bug

Beetle

Mosquito

Moth

Beetle

Mosquito

START

Paste Eggs
Here

Mosquito

Paste Mosquito
Adult Here

Paste
Mosquito
Larva
Here

Paste
Mosquito
Pupa
Here

Moth

Bug

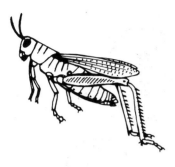

SWIMMING

RUNNING

CLIMBING

JUMPING

DIGGING

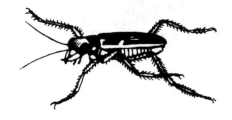

FLYING

LAND OF THE GIANT INSECTS

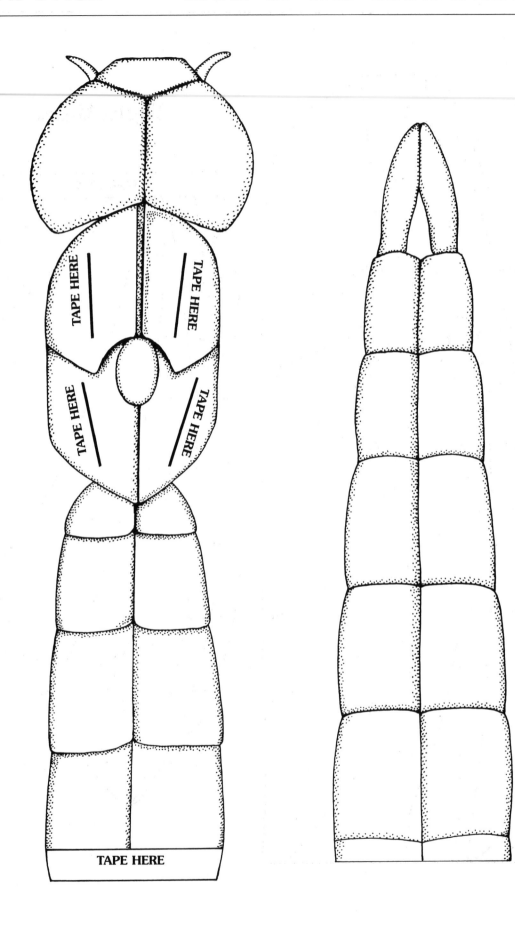

TAPE HERE

TAPE HERE

TAPE HERE

TAPE HERE

TAPE HERE

Right Wing

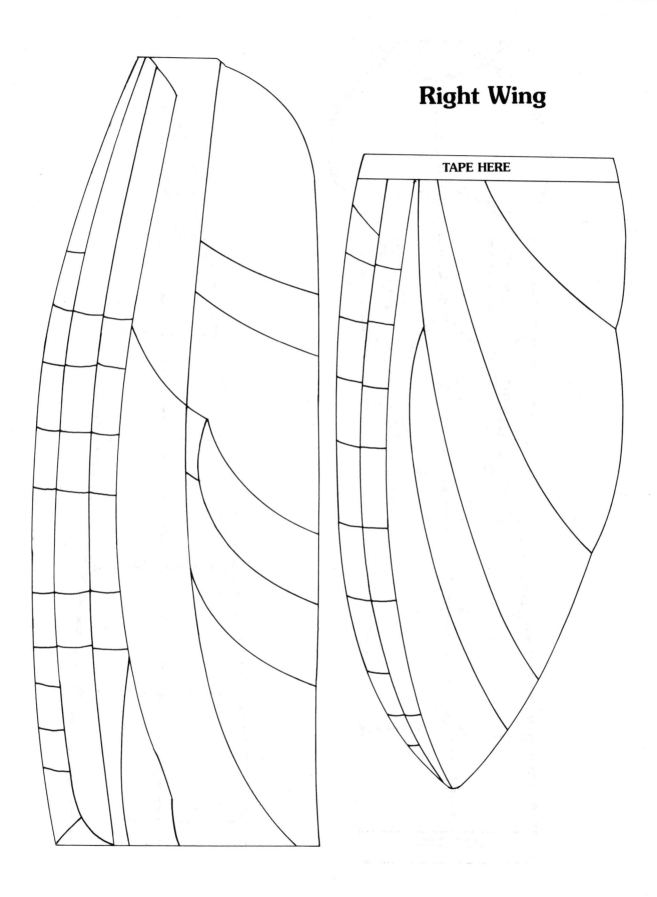

TAPE HERE

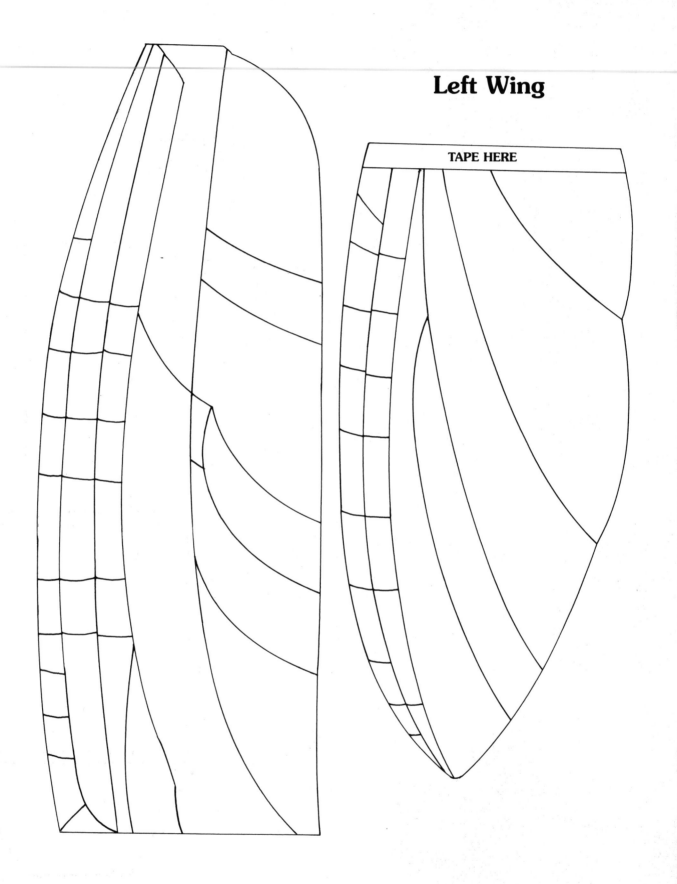

Left Wing

TAPE HERE

LAND AND WATER INSECTS

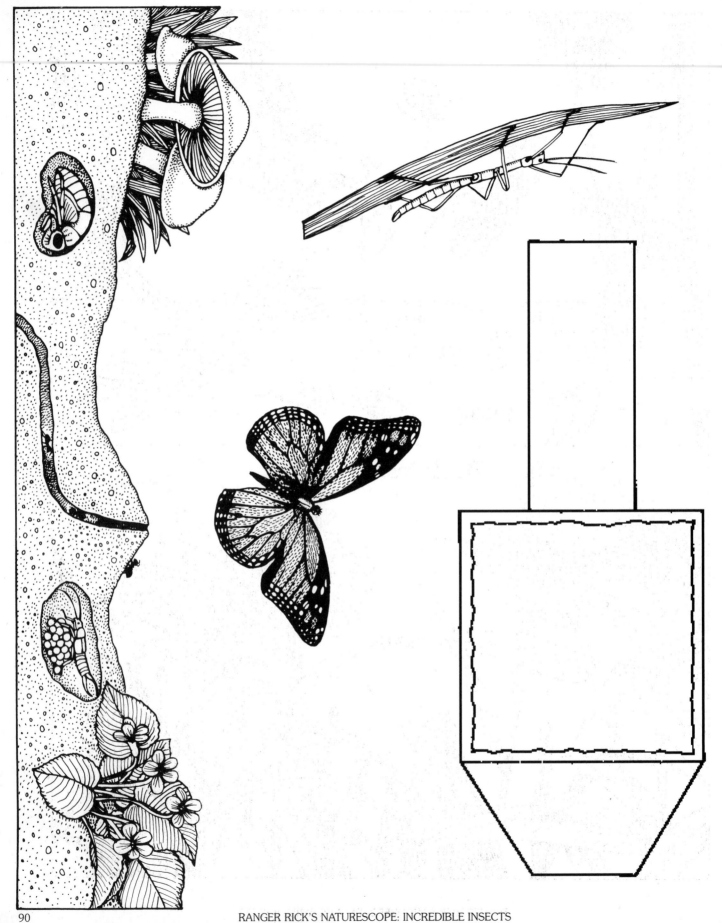

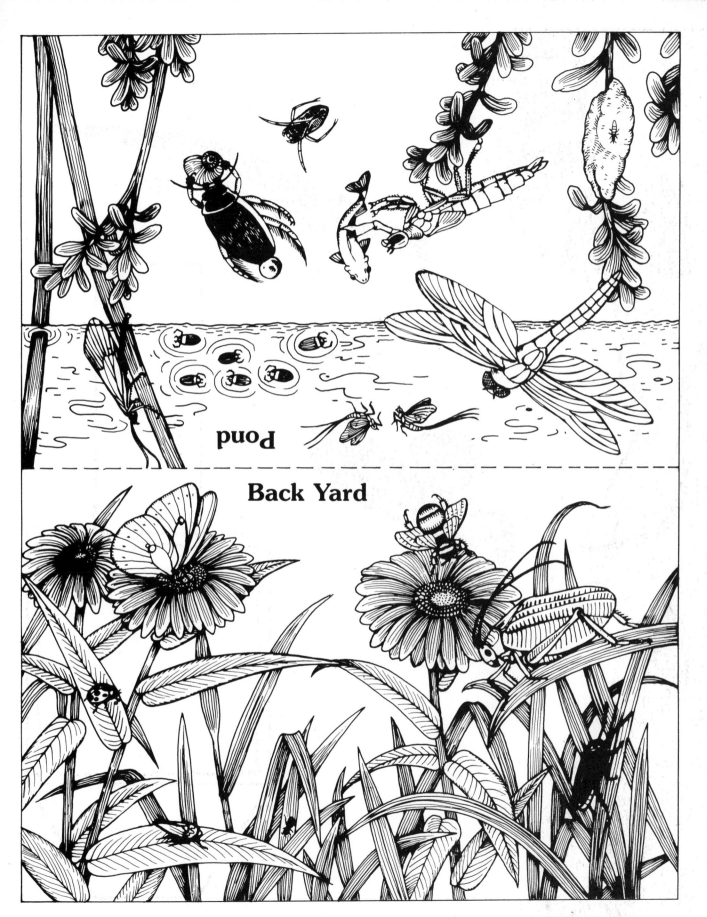

Pond

Back Yard

Bibliography

(Note: A * at the end of a listing indicates that a book is a good source of insect pictures.)

GENERAL REFERENCE BOOKS

The Fascinating World of Beetles by Maria Angels Julivert (Barron's, 1995).*

A Guide To Observing Insect Lives by Donald W. Stokes (Little, Brown, & Co., 1983).

An Inordinate Fondness for Beetles by Arthur V. Evans and Charles L. Bellamy (Henry Holt, 1996).*

An Introduction To the Study of Insects by D.J. Borror, D.M. DeLong, and C.A. Triplehorn (Holt, Rinehart, & Winston, 1976).

Insect by Laurence Mound (Knopf, 1990).*

Insects: Life Cycles and the Seasons by John Brackenbury (Blandford, 1995).*

FIELD GUIDES

The Audubon Society's Field Guide To North American Butterflies by Robert Michael Pyle (Knopf, 1981).*

The Audubon Society's Field Guide To North American Insects and Spiders by L. Milne and M. Milne (Knopf, 1980).*

Butterflies and Moths by R.T. Mitchell and H.S. Zim (Golden Press, 1964).*

A Field Guide to the Insects of America North of Mexico by D.J. Borror and R.E. White (Houghton Mifflin, 1974).*

Insects by H.S. Zim and C. Cottem (Golden Press, 1987).*

Insects is a Nature Finder identification wheel. By turning the wheel, information about different insects is displayed through windows. Available from Hubbard Scientific, 1-800-446-8767.

Peterson First Guides: Insects by Christopher Lechy (Houghton Mifflin, 1987).*

Simon & Schuster's Children's Guide to Insects and Spiders by Jinny Johnson (Simon & Schuster, 1996).*

CHILDREN'S BOOKS

Amazing Bugs Sticker Activity Book (Time-Life, 1997). Primary and Intermediate

Amazing Butterflies and Moths by John Still (Knopf, 1991). Intermediate*

Amazing Insects by Laurence Mound (Knopf, 1993). Primary and Intermediate*

Ant Cities by Arthur Dorros (HarperCollins, 1987). Primary

Big Bugs by Jerry Booth (Harcourt Brace, 1994). Intermediate and Advanced*

Butterflies and Moths by Rosamund Kidman Cox (Usborne, 1990). Primary*

Butterflies and Moths by John Feltwell (Dorling Kindersley, 1997). Primary and Intermediate*

Caterpillar Caterpillar by Vivian French (Candlewick Press, 1995). Primary

Crafts for Kids Who Are Wild About Insects by Kathy Ross (Millbrook Press, 1997). Primary and Intermediate

Fireflies by Caroline Arnold (Scholastic, 1994). Primary

Hornet's Nest by Kate Scarborough (Time-Life, 1997). Primary and Intermediate

I Didn't Know That...Some Bugs Glow in the Dark by Claire Llewellyn (Copper Beach, 1997). Primary and Intermediate

I'd Like To Be an Entomologist by Kim Mitzo Thompson and Karen Mitzo Hilderbrand (Twin Sisters Productions, 1996). Comes with audiocassette. Primary and Intermediate

Insect by Laurence Mound (Knopf, 1990). Advanced*

Insect Lives by Melvin Berger is part of the Ranger Rick's® Science Spectacular series (Newbridge Communications, 1996). Primary and Intermediate. Call 1-800-347-7829 to subscribe to the series.

Insects by Jane Parker (Shooting Star Press, 1993). Intermediate and Advanced*

Insects and Spiders edited by George Else (Time-Life, 1997). Intermediate and Advanced*

Insects Do the Strangest Things by L. and A. Hornblow (Random House, 1990). Intermediate

The Ladybug and Other Insects by Gallimard Jeunesse and Pascale de Bourgoing (Scholastic, 1989). Primary*

Little Giants by Seymour Simon (William Morrow, 1983). Intermediate

The Magic School Bus Gets Ants in Its Pants by Joanna Cole (Scholastic, 1996). Primary

The Magic School Bus Inside a Beehive by Joanna Cole (Scholastic, 1996). Primary

The Very Hungry Caterpillar by E. Carle (Collins & World, 1986). Preschool and Primary

Where Butterflies Grow by Joanne Ryder (Puffin, 1989). Primary

AUDIOCASSETTES AND VIDEOS

Audubon Society's Butterflies for Beginners is a video from MasterVision, 969 Park Ave., New York, NY 10028. Advanced

Bugs! is a video from Time-Life Video, 1-800-621-7026. Intermediate

The Chirping Crickets is a video from Environmental Media, 1-800-368-3382. Intermediate and Advanced.

Lucerne Media offers The Private World of Jean Henri Fabre (Intermediate and Advanced), Praying Mantis (Advanced), and The Wonderful World of the Butterfly (Intermediate and Advanced). Contact Lucerne Media at 37 Ground Pine Rd., Morris Plains, NJ 07950.

The Magic School Bus Gets Ants in Its Pants video by Scholastic, 1-800-SCHOLASTIC. Primary

National Geographic Society offers several insect titles. Butterflies and Insects and How They Grow are Wonders of Learning Kits for primary students that contain student booklets, narration cassette, and teacher's guide with activity sheets. Videos include: Backyard Bugs (all ages), The Benefits of Insects (Intermediate and Advanced), and Dr. Cockroach (Advanced). For more information or to order, call 1-800-368-2728.

The Young Entomologists' Society offers numerous videos as well as replicas of insects, books, and lesson plans. Reach them at 1915 Peggy Pl., Lansing, MI 48910-2253; (517) 887-1499; E-mail: YESbugs@aol.com.

COMPUTER AND ON-LINE RESOURCES

Butterflies of the World is a ZooGuides CD-ROM. Children can view videos and distribution maps, take quizzes, and print out information. For Macintosh and Windows by REMedia, 1-800-573-6334. Intermediate and Advanced

The Butterfly Zone: Your Butterfly Gardening Connection is a colorful Web page including information on how to attract butterflies to your garden, an indentification guide, and a kit to raise painted lady butterflies for eventual release. Visit the site at www.butterflies.com.

Journey North is an Internet-based program that engages students of all ages in a global study of wildlife migration and seasonal change. Student observations of migrating species across the country are shared with other classrooms over the Internet. Children can also follow the work of scientists who are tracking the animals using various technologies. One of the species Journey North participants follow is the monarch butterfly. Participation is free; teachers need only sign up. Teachers can also purchase a packet of supplementary materials, including a 30-page teacher's guide and full-color map. For more information, call (612) 476-6470. Or subscribe at the Journey North Web site—www.learner.org/jnorth.

Learning About Insects is an interactive CD-ROM that contains background information and video clips about insects' life cycles and body structures. For Macintosh and Windows by Queue, 1-800-775-2724. Intermediate

The Multimedia Bug Book is an interactive CD-ROM that allows students to observe more than 50 insects and learn about their habitat and habits. Includes photos, sounds, and video clips designed to help kids build their own "collection" of insects. For Macintosh and Windows. Order from Environmental Media, 1-800-368-3382. Primary and Intermediate

Sim Ant is an educational game in which kids become black ants. They must fight off red ants and run the humans out of their homes to win the game. Along the way, they learn about ant behavior. For Macintosh and Windows from Maxis, 1-800-245-4525. Intermediate and Advanced

OTHER ACTIVITY SOURCES

OBIS (Outdoor Biology Instructional Strategies) Modules published by Delta Education, offers several insect activities that may be purchased separately: *Ants; Bean Bugs; A Better Fly Trap; Bugs, Worms, and Others; Damsels and Dragons; Too Many Mosquitoes;* and *Water Striders.* For more information and to order, call 1-800-258-1302. Intermediate and Advanced

National Science Teachers Association offers numerous activity guides for the study of insects, including *Build Your Own Bugs,* a booklet and set of 29 rubber stamps (Primary and Intermediate); *Creepy Crawlies and the Scientific Method: Over 100 Hands-On Science Experiments* (all ages); *Ladybugs* (Primary); and *The Practical Entomologist* (Intermediate and Advanced). For more information or to order call 1-800-722-NSTA.

Young Entomologists' Society offers Project BUGS (Better Understanding of the Great Sixleggers!), a teaching guide for primary through advanced students. The group also has reference books, insect replicas, information on butterfly gardening, and numerous videos. Reach them at 1915 Peggy Pl., Lansing, MI 48910-2253; (517) 887-1499; E-mail: YESbugs@aol.com

WHERE TO GET MORE INFORMATION

- Beekeepers (check for local associations)
- County extension offices
- Museums, nature centers, state and local parks, zoos
- State department of agriculture, forestry, or natural resources
- College or university departments of entomology
- Web sites:
  The Butterfly Zone http://www.butterflies.com
  Journey North http://www.learner.org/jnorth
  Minibeast World of Insects & Spiders
    http://www.tesser.com/minibeast

Natural Resources

Ranger Rick, published by the National Wildlife Federation, is a monthly nature magazine for elementary-age children.

Ranger Rick® magazine is an excellent source of additional information and activities on insects and many other aspects of nature, outdoor adventure, and the environment. This 48-page award-winning monthly publication of the National Wildlife Federa-tion is packed with the highest-quality color photos, illustrations, and both fiction and nonfiction articles. All factual information in *Ranger Rick* has been checked for accuracy by experts in the field. The articles, games, puzzles, photo-stories, crafts, and other features inform as well as entertain and can easily be adapted for classroom use. To order or for more information, call 1-800-588-1650.

The EarthSavers Club provides an excellent opportunity for you and your students to join thousands of others across the country in helping to improve our environment. Sponsored by Target Stores and the National Wildlife Federation, this program provides children aged 6 to 14 and their adult leaders with free copies of the award-winning *EarthSavers* newspaper and *Activity Guide* four times during the school year, along with a leader's handbook, EarthSavers Club certificate, and membership cards. For more information on how to join, call 1-703-790-4535 or write to EarthSavers; National Wildlife Federation; 8925 Leesburg Pike; Vienna, VA 22184.

Answers to Copycat Pages

Circle the Insect (p. 14)
Insects: 2. grasshopper 3. butterfly 10. caterpillar (swallowtail)
Non-insects: 1. centipede 4. tick 5. scorpion 6. crab 7. spider 8. crayfish 9. millipede

Caterpillar Caper Maze (p. 23)

Insect Match-Up (p. 24)
mosquito—2, house fly—4, monarch butterfly—1, ladybug beetle—5, dragonfly—3

Amazing Insect Mouths (p. 34)
1. butterfly 2. grasshopper 3. mosquito

An Ant's A-mazing World (p. 42)

Growing-Up Word Search (p. 25)

1. moth 2. adult 3. wings 4. butterfly 5. metamorphosis 6. gills 7. egg 8. complete 9. larva 10. simple 11. molt 12. nymph 13. ovipositor 14. caterpillar 15. pupa 16. grub 17. maggot